CHURCH PASTORAL-AID SOCIETY.

Sketch of its Origin and Progress.

———

"*Preach the Word.*"

———

SEELEY, JACKSON, AND HALLIDAY,
FLEET STREET, LONDON.
MDCCCLXXXI.

PREFACE.

A few remarks will suffice to explain the nature of this publication. The need of an authentic narrative of the Society's proceedings, from the date of its institution, had frequently been expressed by many warm friends, and the following pages have been compiled in response to their wishes.

Nearly half a century ago a number of clergy and laity, as will be seen, met together at the Church Missionary House, Salisbury Square, London, for devotion and conference on the subject of "Extending the means of grace in and to necessitous parishes, in strict conformity with the spirit, constitution, and discipline of our venerated Church." It is not too much to say that in the great and glorious work of promoting Evangelical truth in the land the Church Pastoral-Aid Society has, by God's blessing, taken a leading part. It has furnished the means of support to a long succession of faithful clergymen labouring in the overcrowded parishes of our land, and it has moreover successfully contended for the principle of lay-agency, which our Church now generally recognises.

The roll of the Society's founders and earliest supporters contains the names of men who will be

long remembered for their works of faith and labours
of love, their mature wisdom, deep piety, and emi-
nent usefulness. The Society passed through many
trials and difficulties in its early years; it was assailed
as if it were false to the principles of the Church,
and attempts were made to fasten upon it a sectarian
and schismatical character.

The following pages, selected from the minutes and
Quarterly Papers of the Society, present a general
outline of the several stages by which it has risen to
its present prominent position as the handmaid of
the Established Church.

In compiling this record I have been greatly
indebted to the valuable notes and documents of
the energetic Honorary Secretary, Frederic Sandoz,
Esq., which, I regret, could not be further enlarged
upon.

It will not, of course, be forgotten that in
addition to the several speakers at the respective
Anniversaries named in the following sketch, the
Noble President, on each occasion, delivered one of
his long and animated speeches, which were always
listened to with attention by the audience, and
eagerly looked for throughout the country. Lord
Shaftesbury not only showed in these addresses
the value and absolute necessity of the Society's
operations, with which he was well acquainted, in
his philanthropic labours amongst the seething

masses of Lancashire and the northern towns, but
he also fully dwelt on the existing state of things in
the Church of England, which he lamented, and
showed how eminently valuable the Evangelical
principles of the Society were in preserving the
true views of the Established Church. It would
be impossible here fully to record the devoted
labours of the President when, as Lord Ashley, he
took the most constant and active part in the origina-
tion of the Society. His great judgment and counsel
in smoothing down some of the many differences
which were at first felt amongst the friends and
members of the Committee in the formation of its
rules, and bringing things into the order in which
they have ever since continued, cannot be over-
estimated. From the earliest moment to the present,
he has taken the liveliest interest in the work of the
Society, and has scarcely ever been absent from the
chair at the Annual Meetings. All its supporters
fervently hope that his Lordship may long be spared,
not only to preside over its Anniversaries, but to
afford the Committee his kind and wise counsel in
any season of difficulty which may arise.

His Lordship's fervent and weighty words uttered
in May last deserve to be borne in mind when he
said :—"Let me implore of you to persevere in the
work in which you have begun, so that when the
day of attack shall have arrived (and that day may
not be far distant), you may be able to say that you

have exhibited in the cause of God and His Church more vigour, more devotion, more love for the truth, more life, and more of the spirit of prayer, than you have ever done at any preceding period."

It is with deep thankfulness and renewed hope that the Committee render praise to Him who has "led them these" more than "forty years," and caused the Society to "lack nothing" of spiritual blessing.

EDWARD J. SPECK, M.A.,
Clerical Secretary.

TEMPLE CHAMBERS, FALCON COURT,
  FLEET STREET, LONDON, E.C.

    9th February, 1881.

CHURCH PASTORAL-AID SOCIETY.

Sketch of its Origin and Progress.

Instituted in the year 1836 for the purpose of bene-fiting the population of our own country by increasing the number of working clergymen in the Church of England, and encouraging the employment of pious and discreet laymen as helpers to the clergy in duties not ministerial.

<hr>

LETTER OF MR. FREDERIC SANDOZ.

ON the 12th of February, 1836, the following letter, signed " F. S.," which there is reason to believe was from Frederic Sandoz, Esq., was addressed to the *Record* newspaper :—

"CHURCH PASTORAL-AID SOCIETY.

"TO THE EDITOR OF THE RECORD.

"Sir,—It will afford you and many of your readers satisfaction to hear that the above-named Society will, it is hoped, under the favour of God, be instituted on Friday next, the 19th instant; and the prayerful will, we trust, bear it on their hearts in the interval, entreating

B

the Lord, ' from whom all holy desires, all good counsels, and all just works do proceed,' to bless it as a means to the promotion of His glory in the welfare of souls. The promoters have simply relied on the Lord to guide them hitherto, and, in that course which it is proposed to adopt, believe they see His hand and way. Oh! that the wealthy and zealous members of our Church may come forward with liberal and self-denying contributions ; and we then doubt not, through trust in God, that a brief experience will abundantly evidence to all the great *need* and the great *blessing* of such a Society. The earliest possible assistance will be highly appreciated, and with hearty thanks for yours,

" I am, Sir, your most obedient servant,
"Islington, Feb. 12, 1836."   "F. S.

Accordingly at a meeting of clergy and laity held on Friday, the 19th of February, 1836, at the Church Missionary House, Salisbury Square, Fleet S'reet, the Rev. Josiah Pratt read a statement, together with certain proposed regulations for the Society, to be submitted for adoption to a general meeting of about seventy of the clergy and laity, which was accordingly held at one o'clock on the same day and at the same place, in pursuance of the following circular letter of invitation :—

" *Church Pastoral-Aid Society.*

" Sir,—Having regard to the true interests of our National Church, as well as to the spiritual welfare of multitudes who are wholly or greatly deprived of her pastoral care, and consequent on several communications with and from esteemed individuals among the clergy and laity, the promoters of the Church Pastoral-Aid

Society have determined, in humble hope of the Divine blessing, to convene a meeting of the friends of the object, for which occasion the use of the committee-room of the Church Missionary Society has been kindly granted.

"We have accordingly most earnestly to solicit the favour of your attendance at the Church Missionary House, Salisbury Square, Fleet Street, on Friday, the 19th instant, at one o'clock precisely, when a plan for extending the means of grace in and to necessitous parishes in strict conformity with the spirit, constitution, and discipline of our venerated Church will be submitted, which it is trusted will meet with your cordial approval and strenuous support.

"Entreating your prayers for a special blessing on the design and occasion,

    "We are, with Christian regards,
            "Yours most faithfully,
    "JOSIAH PRATT, B.D., Vicar of St. Stephen's,
            Coleman Street.
    "THOMAS SNOW, M.A., Rector of St. Dunstan's,
            Fleet Street.
    "THOMAS DALE, M.A., Vicar of St. Bride's, Fleet
            Street.
    "ROBERT SEELEY, 172, Fleet Street.
    "FREDERIC SANDOZ, 30, Park Place West, } Hon.
            Islington.   } Secs.
    "NADIR BAXTER, 12, Brompton Square."   }

At this Meeting Lord Ashley occupied the chair, and there were present—

The Revs. Josiah Pratt, Thomas Snow, Thomas Dale, J. M. Rodwell, Cornwall Smalley, William Thompson, Thomas Watson, H. B. Hill, Roxby Maude, F. Dollman, A. S. Thelwall, R. C. Dillon, J. R. Barber, Henry Davies, D. Ruell, M. M. Preston, J. Haslegrave,

B 2

J. Ellaby, J. Nott, T. M. Fallow, E. Blick, J. Pratt, jun., William Jowett and — Grimstead; Viscount Midleton, Sir Andrew Agnew, Bart, M.P.; John Hardy, Esq., M.P.; Alexander Pringle, Esq., M.P.; Hon. Captain F. Maude, Colonel Phipps; Messrs. John Bridges, M. Hornidge, R. Seeley, D. Coates, H. Cox, W. Harding, C. Brodrick, G. Baxter, J. Nisbet, J. Spurling, W. Leach, T. Thompson, — Smith, R. McCulloch, E.V. Sidebottom, W. Dugmore, W. Malton, J.C. Colquhoun, H. C. Christian, W. Pitman, Samuel Hanson, T. G. Conyers, W. S. Hale, J. Deacon, Dr. John Whiting, — Young; John Labouchere, Treasurer of the Society. Rev. John Harding (afterwards Bishop of Bombay), N. Baxter, and Fred. Sandoz, Esquires, Honorary Secretaries.

The Rev. Thomas Snow opened the Meeting with prayer.

The Revs. Josiah Pratt, Thomas Snow, and Mr. Fred. Sandoz severally stated the circumstances under which they felt called upon to unite with other clergymen and laymen who were anxious for the formation of a Society on the principles and grounds set forth in a statement annexed.

Letters received from clergy and laity in many parts of the country testifying to the need and desire for such an institution, were then presented, together with three to the same effect from the Lord Bishop of Chester, containing valuable suggestions and counsel, with an assurance of his Lordship's gladly availing himself of any aid which the Society might be able to offer to his Diocese.

Letters were also received from the Revs. Dr.
Dealtry, Edward Bickersteth, H. Higginson,
Robert Monro, and others, expressing regret that
important prior engagements prevented their
attendance at the Meeting, on which they desired
God's blessing.

It was then, on the Motion of John Hardy,
Esq., M.P., seconded by John Labouchere, Esq.,
Resolved—

" That a Society be formed, to be called ' The Church
Pastoral-Aid Society,' and that the following be the
regulations and constitution of the Society, subject to
such addition or modification as may appear advisable
to the Committee at their first Meeting, prior to publication." *

On the Motion of Alexander Pringle, Esq.,
M.P., seconded by William Dugmore, Esq., Resolved—

" That the statement now read be adopted, and circulated, under the direction of the Committee."

On the Motion of J. C. Colquhoun, Esq.,
seconded by John Bridges, Esq., Resolved—

" That John Labouchere, Esq., be requested to act as
Treasurer of this Society."

On the Motion of John Deacon, Esq., seconded
by William Leach, Esq., Resolved—

" That the following gentlemen be of the Committee,
with power to extend their number to twenty-four:—
Right Hon. Lord Ashley, M.P., John Hardy, Esq., M.P.,

* Such as they now appear in the Annual Report.

Sir Oswald Mosley, M.P., Abel Smith, Esq., M.P., Sir Walter Farquhar, J. P. Plumptre, Esq., M.P., H. Blanchard, John Bridges, J. Spurling, William Dugmore, Harry Cox, W. H. Mayne, Hugh Hill, George Hambleton, Marmaduke Hornidge, William Pitman, George Friend, H. C. Christian, R. McCulloch, Esquires. Fred. Sandoz and Nadir Baxter, Esquires, Honorary Secretaries."

On the Motion of Dandeson Coates, Esq., seconded by Nadir Baxter, Esq., Resolved—

"That the respectful acknowledgments of this Meeting be presented to the Right Hon. Lord Ashley, M.P., for his kindness in taking the chair this day, and for the able manner in which he has conducted the business of the Meeting."

The First Annual Report contained the following statement respecting the meetings of committees: "The Committee will here state, that the General Committee meet at the Society's office the first Thursday in every month, at one o'clock, or oftener, as required; and that no grants of aid nor important measure can be adopted without the approval of the General Committee, of which all subscribing clergymen are members, and to which those resident in London and its vicinity are summoned. They have found it necessary to appoint from their body a Sub-Committee of Management and Preliminary Correspondence, consisting of twelve clergymen and twelve laymen, whose meetings, with breakfast, shall be held every Tuesday morning at eight o'clock, and oftener, as required."

FIRST COMMITTEE MEETING.

The first meeting of the Committee of the Society was held at the Chambers, Falcon Court, Fleet Street, on the 17th of March, 1836. The following members were present :—

John Twells, Esq., in the chair. The Revs. Blick, Barber, Dale, Haslegrave, Knell, Lane, Pratt, jun., J. Rodwell, Sandys, Snow, Thelwall, Woodward ; Messrs. Bicknell, Clarke, Cobb, Conyers, Cox, Deverell, Harcourt, Hornidge, Lewin, McCulloch, Pitman, Seeley, and Spurling. Rev. J. Harding (late Bishop of Bombay), N. Baxter, and F. Sandoz, Honorary Secretaries.

The Committee avowed their conviction that it was the bounden duty of the Legislature of a Christian land to provide means out of the National resources for the religious instruction and welfare of the country ; and expressed their belief that much of the apathy which existed on this subject was traceable to the great deficiency of Church accommodation and of other provision for the pastoral care of the people who could not be expected to feel their need in this respect until they had been brought by the means of grace, and through the ordinances of the Church, to admit their value and benefit.

In the statement of the Society's design adopted

by the constituent meeting of the 19th February, 1836, the following paragraph occurs :—

" The founders of the Society are well aware that there are circumstances in these times which may justly cause the authorities of the Church to hesitate in taking the lead in new plans until their beneficial bearing and direction shall have been sufficiently ascertained. On this account they do not ask, for the present, any avowed patronage of that description, fully satisfied that the Society will receive such countenance and support when it shall be seen that the simple principle of supplying to the clergy greater means of usefulness in the discharge of their recognised duties opens a wide field of orderly and beneficial action."

The Committee observed that their plan was not prosecuted without due regard to Episcopal sanction, " which the members of the Church of England must ever deem authoritative and of essential importance in carrying on with vigour and efficiency any design which relates to the extension of her usefulness and influence."

After full deliberation, an outline plan of the Society was accordingly submitted to the most reverend the archbishops, and some of the right reverend the bishops, with a respectful request that if any objection or suggestion occurred to their Lordships the honour of a communication might be conferred, the single desire of the promoters of the plan being to afford aid to the clergy of that Church of which they were attached

members, and for the increased efficiency and
stability of which they were ready to devote their
best efforts.

NECESSITY OF LAY AGENCY—DUTIES OF A LAY ASSISTANT.

The necessity of lay agency is distinctly affirmed
in the original Statement, Constitution, and Regulations of the Society as follows :—" It is by such
an agency, in great measure, that the mass of the
people are to be brought by God's blessing to
become willing and desirous to place themselves
under the ministry of the Word."   The office of
lay assistant is thus described : " The lay assistant
is to be considered as a visitor of families, not as
taking upon himself the office of a public instructor ; to be in subordination to the incumbent,
leading people to frequent the house of God, and
thus filling the churches already built, or creating
a desire and necessity for others." The Committee
deprecated any assumption of the ministerial office
by such officers, as appeared from the following
extract from a paper intended to explain the position in which the lay assistants were placed, to be
put into the hands of every layman engaging in
the service of the Society :—

*" Remember that your business is to be simply this :
the visiting from day to day the people of the district in
which you are placed for the purpose of inquiring into
their spiritual state, conversing with them on the things*

of God, entreating their attention by solemn but affectionate persuasion to the care of their souls, and, in one word, seeking by all scriptural means to bring them to Christ."

And, again :—

" You are to look to the minister with whom the Society places you for direction in all your plans, employing no methods for the spiritual welfare of the people without his sanction, remembering that, according to the order of that Church which Providence hath established amongst us, the pastoral care of souls is, we believe, committed by Christ to the parochial minister; that he is the responsible party; and that your course, therefore, is to be shaped entirely by his conscientious judgment of what is right. At such times as he shall require you will be ready to give to him a particular report in writing of all your proceedings."

The Society therefore proposed the employment, *when sufficient clerical assistance could not be obtained,* of duly qualified laymen to act in subordination to the incumbent, and under his direction and control.

DIFFICULTIES REGARDING LAY AGENCY.

Difficulties with regard to the principle of lay agency early beset the Society. It was felt that they might be removed under the consentaneous encouragement of the bishops and by co-operation of the parochial clergy. The Committee stated it to be of primary importance that the authority of the bishop in every diocese, and of the incumbent as the responsible minister in every parish, should be maintained. The lay assistants were to be in nowise responsible to the Society or under its control, but wholly subordinate to the incumbent of the parish or district in which they were placed.

It was thought that among the class of laymen specially available to this end would be candidates for holy orders, many of whom often completed their university course before they were of age for ordination. At the same time, it was clearly seen that from this source would be gathered but a limited number of the assistants required, and that others must be sought for. In some parishes the lay assistant might devote his whole time, in others a portion of his time. The opinion of the Committee on these points was thus set forth in the Seventh Regulation, " The Society will assist, as it may be able, in the supply to destitute places, of lay agents, whether candidates for holy orders or others, or whether partially or wholly to be maintained, which lay agent shall act under the direction of the incumbent, and be removed by him at his pleasure."

LETTERS OF REVS. C. BENSON AND W. CARUS.

.To this regulation exception was taken by several friends of the Society, who desired to limit lay agency to candidates for orders. The Rev. Christopher Benson, Master of the Temple, wrote :

"The Society will have, in my opinion, more supporters if lay agency is strictly confined to candidates for orders, or rather, if the Society only furnished clerical assistants, and aided in procuring places of worship." The Rev. W. Carus, Senior Fellow of Trinity College, Cambridge, wrote :—" The good you will then do (*i.e.*, in the event of alteration in Regulation) will be incomparably greater than on the present system. The bishops beginning in every diocese to patronize you." Certain friends at Derby also expressed the opinion that the Society's aid should be limited to lay graduates and clergymen.

COMMITTEE UNWILLING TO ABANDON OR LIMIT LAY AGENCY.

The Committee then stated the grounds on which they felt precluded from recommending any abandonment or limitation of lay agency, as follow :—"A fundamental object of this Society is to afford such aid to the clergy in the discharge of their duties as they may be desirous to accept, and a fundamental principle of the Society is to respect the judgment and choice, liberty and responsibility of the incumbents of parishes, subject as they are to the authority of their Bishops in regard to the agency proper to be employed in bringing the population committed to their charge to the knowledge of the

" truth as it is in Jesus." The Society, therefore, does not presume to dictate to incumbents whether they shall have clerical or lay assistance, but on their application for either, the Committee is to consider the circumstances of the case and determine thereon, according to their ability, with due regard to the funds of the Society, and to the necessities of the parish or district. " In recognising lay agency the Society innovated in no respect, seeing that the employment of pious laymen, in subordination to the minister of the Gospel, obtained in apostolic times, has prevailed in successive ' ages, is recognised by the officers and constitution of the mother Church, and has been extensively sanctioned by the Society for Promoting Christian Knovledge, the Society for the Propagation of the Gospel, and other Church Societies in the Mission of Catechists to the colonies and heathen lands."

The Committee also received testimonies to the value of such agency as well from the clergy, who had employed it through the aid of the Society, as from other experienced and faithful ministers of the Church.   The great bulk of the supporters of the Society were, it was apprehended, also decidedly in favour of affording aid to the clergy who were desirous of employing pious laymen under their own direction and control in promoting the spiritual as well as temporal

welfare of the many neglected and ignorant portions of our population in large and necessitous
parishes.

Having regard, then, to the objects and principles of this Society, to the responsibility of the
clergy, to the practice of the Church, to the experience of the incumbents, and to good faith with
the supporters of the Society, the Committee felt
unable to adopt any measure which should, either
directly or indirectly, impugn the principle of lay
agency, or infringe the sacred liberty and solemn
responsibility of each bishop and each incumbent
relatively to determine on the means for religious
instruction proper to be employed in his diocese
or parish respectively, or prevent associated individuals from affording aid to promote the welfare
and efficiency of the Church in any manner which
is in accordance with the spirit of her laws and
the great end of her institution.

COMMITTEE DISPOSED TO SOME MODIFICATIONS.

The Committee, however, were disposed to modification in the practice of the Society, and to
embody it in a regulation, which might go far to
meet the objections of some, and at the same
time maintain the above principles.

They considered that it would be expedient to
abstain from all direct engagement by the Society
of the persons to be employed by the clergy, and,

as at present, from all direction and control of such
persons, only requiring from the applicant that
full satisfaction be given to the Committee that a
case proposed was such as to justify the Committee
in rendering the aid of the Society.   This course
would avoid some difficulties and expense connected
with stipendiary engagements made by the Society,
and would at the same time remove the objection
entertained and the danger apprehended by some
consequent on a voluntary Society centralizing
lay agency and having a Mission of lay assistants,
while it would in no way restrict the Society in
affording aid to incumbents who might consider
such agency essential to the well-being of the
population committed to their charge.   The
Society would then devolve the whole responsibility on the clergy, and leave the question of the
necessity and fitness of using lay assistants in the
opinion of high authorities in the Church and of
this Committee, to be left with those to whom is
committed the care of souls, and who must judge
for themselves what means are to be employed by
them in the execution of their high charges, re-
strained of course by the laws of the Church of
England of which they were ministers.

The following addition was directed to be made
to the Regulations of the Society :—

"*No grant from the Society can be made unless
the incumbent himself shall apply or sanction the*

application for assistance, the Committee only claim-
ing sufficient proof of the exigencies of the case and
full satisfaction as to the sentiments and character
of the persons proposed to be employed. Such per-
sons when approved shall be under engagement as
well as entire responsibility to the incumbent or
other clergyman employing them. The grants of
the Society shall be made for one year subject
to renewal."

OBJECTIONS OF SOME BISHOPS.

Reference is made in the above preamble to
" the danger apprehended by some consequent on
a voluntary Society centralising lay agency and
having a Mission of lay assistants." In the
opinion of several of the Bishops, the Society in-
fringed in a great degree on the discipline of the
United Church; an infringement which, it was
urged, was in no respect palliated by the necessity
of the case, since in all instances of spiritual destitution the object of the Society might be attained
by a clerical agent with at least equal efficiency,
and, it was believed, without any increase of expenditure.

Others affirmed that while the employment of
lay agency was recognised by all attached members of the United Church, many, and among
them some of the highest authorities in the
Church, to whom " an enlightened respect " was
due, were opposed, not to the efforts of laymen for

the spiritual welfare of those around them, but
to the introduction into the Church of a new and
distinct order of lay teachers, the stipendiaries of
a voluntary Society and in no respect amenable
to ecclesiastical authority.

Also that by the second Regulation of the Society, the religious influence of the United Church
is to be promoted by such methods only as are in
entire consistency with her discipline and order,
and that no method can be in accordance with
the spirit of this Regulation which is opposed to
the known and express sentiments of many among
the appointed conservators and guardians of that
order and discipline.

OPINIONS OF BISHOPS OF EXETER AND LONDON.

The Bishop of Exeter (Dr. Phillpotts), who, at
the first, had written expressing his entire approval of the Society's objects and plan, at this
juncture withdrew from the Society. He thus
wrote :—" If an incumbent shall, from the circumstances of his parish, feel it necessary to use the
assistance of laymen in instructing the more ignorant of his flock, it can hardly happen but that
among his own parishioners he will find those
who will give him the aid he needs. The introduction for this purpose of a regular salaried lay
officer, sent from a distance by an irresponsible
Society, and not even amenable directly and legally

to the Bishop, is, in my estimation, highly objectionable." The Bishop of London (Dr. Blomfield) also wrote, expressing his desire that the Society's aid should be limited to clerical assistance.

The Committee, in consequence of the views thus expressed, decided to submit the following Resolution, to be substituted for the Seventh Regulation :—" *That applications be received by this Society for clerical assistance only, and that they be addressed by the incumbent to the Committee, accompanied with the requisite information concerning the character of the individual to be employed, and the amount of additional service to be performed ; but that no grant shall take effect until the proposed object of its appropriation shall have been communicated by the applicant to the Bishop of the Diocese.*"

At an adjourned Special General Committee held on the 16th of February, 1837, it was resolved to submit the following addition to the Society's Regulations at the next meeting of the General Committee :—" *No grant from the Society can be made unless the incumbent himself shall apply or sanction the application for assistance ; the Committee only claiming sufficient proof of the exigencies of the case, and full satisfaction as to the sentiments and character of the persons to be em-*

ployed. Such persons, when approved, shall be under engagement, as well as entire responsibility, to the incumbent or other clergyman employing them. The grants of the Society shall be made for one year subject to renewal."

LETTERS OF CANON ROGERS, BISHOP OF CHESTER, AND LORD ASHLEY.

Letters were read from the following, amongst others, on the subject of the proposed limitations regarding lay agency, as well as its entire renunciation. The Rev. Canon Rogers, of Exeter, wrote to the President soliciting a reconsideration of the question of lay agency, with a view to its entire renunciation, or at least its limitation to graduates, candidates for holy orders. Canon Rogers' letter to be submitted to the General Committee.

At a meeting of the General Committee, held on the 6th of April, 1837, letters were read from the Lord Bishop of Chester (Dr. Sumner) and Lord Ashley, urging the importance of a declaratory Minute to be published by the Committee, with reference to their practice in future grants of aid for the employment of lay assistants.

FIRST ANNIVERSARY.

The First Annual Meeting of the Society was held in the small room, Exeter Hall, on Monday the 9th of May, 1836, the Right Hon. Lord Ashley in the chair. The speakers were the Right Rev.

c 2

the Lord Bishop of Chester, the Very Rev. the
Dean of Armagh, the Dean of Clogher, Rev. Dr.
Dealtry; Revs. C. Dukinfield, Thomas V. Short,
Thomas Snow, Hugh Stowell; Messrs. Richard
Alsager, William Garratt, and·John Weylland.

The Resolutions deplored the state of spiritual
destitution prevailing in many parts of the country,
and recognised with much satisfaction the principles on which the Society proceeded, and its
mode of meeting that destitution. The Committee
referred to public documents of unquestionable
authority, which revealed the appalling fact that
100,000 souls, in spite of every effort, national
and voluntary, were annually added to those who
in Protestant England, and under the wing of an
Established Church, had neither pastors, nor sacraments, nor public worship, nor any of the habits
of religion, but were left unheeded, with no man
to care for their souls. Under such circumstances
it became the imperative duty of every right-
hearted Christian and Churchman to come forward that he might promote, according to the
fundamental regulations of the Society, "the religious influence of the Church by such methods
only as it may be competent to a voluntary Society
to employ in entire consistency with her discipline
and order."

LETTER OF MR. SANDOZ TO BISHOP OF LONDON.

Mr. Frederic Sandoz, in the course of a letter dated the 23rd of January, 1836, to the Lord Bishop of London (Dr. Blomfield), had observed:—" The great necessity for pastoral-aid in other parts than the metropolis, and in other dioceses than London, must be well known to your Lordship, and evidenced to be deeply felt by the success of the appeals made by Dissenters and by others, irrespective of ecclesiastical regularity, and there are many Churchmen who, if the Pastoral-Aid Society cannot speedily be established, will, rather than do nothing, set about the formation of a Society to employ laymen to read the Liturgy of the Church in public worship and to preach the Gospel, declaring themselves not to be Dissenters but Churchmen."

The first sermon before the Society was preached on the 11th of May, 1836, at the parish church of St. Bride's, Fleet Street, London, by the Rev. Hugh Stowell, Minister of Christ Church, Salford, from the words of the Gospel, St. Luke xiv. 23. The first Occasional Paper of the Society was published in July, 1836, and contained extracts from the letters of several clergymen applying for aid, and stating the condition of their parishes; also a statement and appeal from the Committee calling attention to the great necessity for forming local associations, and giving information with regard to the funds of the Society. The following regulations appeared in the " Occasional Notes " for July :—

REGULATIONS.

1. The Society shall be designated the Church Pastoral-Aid Society.

2. The object of this Society shall be to promote the religious influence of the United Church by such methods only as it may be competent to a voluntary society to employ in entire consistency with her discipline and order.

3. That with this view authentic and exact information shall be sought relative to such portions of the population as may be most destitute of religious instruction, and such aid rendered to the clergy in the discharge of their duties as they may be desirous to accept, and the Society may have it in their power to render; no aid being given except so far as local exertions shall be found to be incompetent to the necessities of the case.

4. That the assistance to be rendered by the Society shall respect either places of worship or labourers under the direction of the incumbents of parishes or districts.

5. That in destitute places where no other sufficient means are available, the Society will assist, according to its power, in appropriating as places of worship and for the administration of the Word

of God, buildings already erected, or in erecting churches or chapels for that end.

6. That the Society will contribute such help as may be in its power to the support of additional clergymen in destitute parishes or districts, who shall zealously and faithfully co-operate with the incumbent.

7. That the Society will assist, as it may be able, in the supply to destitute places of lay agents, whether candidates for holy orders or others, or whether partially or wholly to be maintained; which lay agents shall act under the direction of the incumbent, and be removable at his pleasure.

8.* No grant from the Society's funds for the benefit of any parish or district can be made unless the incumbent himself shall apply or sanction the application for aid, and shall furnish to the Committee sufficient proof of the exigencies of the case. The nomination of an assistant shall always be left with the clergyman to whom id is given, the Committee claiming only full satisfaction as to the qualifications of his nominee, who, when approved, will be under engagement only to the clergyman by whom he is employed, and solely responsible to him. Grants from the Society towards the support of an assistant are

* This Regulation was adopted on the 18th of April, 1837.

made to the clergyman to whom aid is given, and are voted for one year.

The second. Occasional Paper was issued in November, 1836, and contained (1) A Minute of the Committee, (2) Extracts from the Correspondence of the Society, (3) Statement of the Committee.

In April, 1837, a Resolution was passed, expressing deep regret at the decease of the Bishops of Salisbury and Norwich, Vice-Patrons of the Society.

SECOND ANNIVERSARY.

The Second Anniversary Meeting of the Society was held at the Freemasons' Hall, Great Queen Street, on the 12th May, 1837, Lord Ashley in the Chair, supported by the Bishops of Chester and Winchester. The speakers were the Bishops of Chester and Winchester, the Revs. H. Stowell, C. Lane, H. Raikes, H. R. Roxby, Thomas Snow, and D. Wilson ; Messrs. W. A. Garratt and J. Labouchere (Treasurer of the Society).

The income of the Society from the date of its institution to the 31st of March, 1837, was 7,363*l*., but of this sum only about 1,800*l*. appeared as annual subscriptions. The Committee trusted that many sums contributed as donations would be continued yearly, and that the list of subscribers would also receive large augmentation, inasmuch as upon annual contributors the Committee must

depend for the renewal of their grants from year
to year, according as the exigencies of the several
cases should require.   It was stated that the
grants already voted amounted to nearly 4,500*l.*,
and that in almost every case the renewal of those
grants would be most urgently desired.   The
Committee observed that every friend of the
Society would be sensible of the urgent necessity
for vigorous and extended efforts in order to
increase the means at their disposal.   They
trusted that the clergy especially would, in their
respective neighbourhoods, consider in what way
they might be best able to promote the cause of
the Society.

CONSTITUTION OF SUB-COMMITTEE—ADDITIONAL REGULATION.

The Sub or Working Committee, consisting of
twelve lay and twelve clerical members, the latter
of whom had the additional important duties of
considering the nominations of curates and lay-
assistants, on the 6th of April, 1837, recommended
to the next General Committee the adoption of the
following additional Regulation :—

" *No grant from the Society's funds for the
benefit of any parish or district can be made unless
the incumbent himself shall apply, or sanction the
application for aid, and shall furnish to the Committee sufficient proof of the exigencies of the case.
The nomination of an assistant shall always be left*

with the clergyman to whom the aid is given, the Committee claiming only full satisfaction as to the qualifications of his nominee, who, when approved, will be under engagement only to the clergyman by whom he is employed, and solely responsible to him. Grants from the Society towards the support of an assistant are made to the clergyman to whom aid is given, and are voted for one year."

BISHOP OF EXETER PREFERS "CLERGY-AID SOCIETY."

Letters from friends, more or less averse from the principle of lay agency, or desirous that limitations should be set thereto, continued to flow in. The Bishop of Exeter (Dr. Phillpotts) wrote that he preferred the Clergy-Aid Society, " especially as it is free from an objection to which, under any modifications, the employment of laymen as recognised assistants in a permanent character can hardly fail to be exposed."

RESOLUTION OF NORWICH LOCAL COMMITTEE.

It was felt by some that more stringent regulations should be adopted respecting the examination into the character and experience of those to be employed as lay-assistants. The following Resolution of the Norwich local Committee was submitted to the Parent Committee in London :—
" That the Committee of the Norwich Auxiliary beg to recommend to the Committee of the Parent Society that no lay-assistant be engaged without

first undergoing personal examination by the
clerical referees of the Parent Society, in conformity with the sixteen questions under the head
of lay-assistants." The Clerical Committee of the
4th July, 1837, reported to the Sub-Committee
that it was highly desirable that the Committee
should, for the future, encourage the engagement
of such laymen as having other occupation and
means of subsistence, might be employed for a
limited portion of their time, and at a small
remuneration, under the superintendence of the
parochial clergyman, in the performance of whatever duties he might assign. The Committee of
6th of July, 1837, concurred in the above recom-
mendation.

The general feeling of the Committee at this
time appeared to be in favour of clerical above
lay agency, while the Society provided for the
latter, where considered desirable.

The Second Annual Sermon before the Society
was preached in the Church of St. Clement
Danes, Strand, London, on Thursday, 11th May,
1837, by the Rev. John Norman Pearson, M.A.,
Principal of the Church Missionary Institution,
and Sunday Evening Lecturer of St. Mary's,
Islington, from 2 Cor. iv. 1.

In this year the Society made 110 grants to 100
incumbents; viz., 92 for curates and 18 for lay
assistants. The aggregate population under the

charge of these clergymen was 869,977, giving an average of 8,699 to each. The incomes of these incumbents averaged only 157*l.* each, and 46 of them were unprovided with either a glebe-house or parsonage.

THIRD ANNIVERSARY.

The Third Annual Meeting was held in the large room, Exeter Hall, on the 8th of May, 1838, Lord Ashley in the chair. The Rev. J. Harding, Honorary Secretary, read the Report, which referred to certain cases of aid afforded in the past year by the Society, also to the appointment of a Clerical Stipendiary Secretary, which had become indispensable, as the business hitherto conducted by Honorary Secretaries, notwithstanding their great devotedness, had extended to a degree which rendered it impossible for them to retain so important an office without further assistance. These gentlemen expressed their willingness still to take a part in serving the cause of the Society.

The Rev. William Pullen was, by the unanimous vote of the Committee, appointed Travelling Secretary of the Society. The speakers at the Meeting were the Bishop of Winchester, Lord Sandon, the Revs. H. Stowell, Marsh, and others. The Third Annual Sermon was preached at St. Bride's Church, Fleet Street, London, on the 7th of May, 1838, by the Bishop of Chester, afterwards Archbishop of Canterbury, upon the text Ezek. xxxiv. 6.

"A VOICE FROM THE FONT."

The publication, in 1838, of a book, entitled "A Voice from the Font," originally printed in the *Church Quarterly Review* for October of that year, occasioned much discussion in the Committee. The Revs. J. Kidd and Hugh Stowell directed the attention of the Committee to the following extract from this article, containing statements characterized by them as most injurious to the interests of the Society :—

" An incumbent of a populous town in the West of England applied for two lay teachers, who were granted, but who, after establishing an acquaintance and intimacy with the parishioners, became Dissenting ministers of the town, drawing to them those whom they had visited and taught as the delegates of the incumbent."

The Secretary was instructed by the Committee to write to Messrs. Longman, the publishers of the *Church Quarterly Review*, on the subject. Messrs. Longman replied, stating that the author of "A Voice from the Font" had desired the note on p. 29 to be pasted over in the remaining copies of that work, with which they should comply.

Speculation was rife as to the author of the book, and the Rev. J. Simpson, of Newark, wrote, referring to the Ven. Archdeacon Wilkins, of Nottingham, as the individual in question. The Rev. J. Harding was instructed to write to the

Ven. Archdeacon Wilkins to know if he be the author.

A letter was received on the 11th of December, 1838, from the Editor of the *Church of England Quarterly Review*, stating that he would willingly have retracted the false statement which had appeared in the Review respecting the Society, but that such statement being a mere quotation, for which the author alone is responsible, he cannot undertake to do so. It was decided to insert an explanatory advertisement, accompanied with a synopsis of the Society, in the *Church of England Quarterly Review*.

REASON OF DISAGREEMENT AND FORMATION OF ADDITIONAL CURATES SOCIETY.

" The ground of disagreement which alienated the High Church party from the Church Pastoral-Aid Society and induced them to commence a rival Institution was this :—The Committee of the Church Pastoral-Aid Society said, 'We are entrusted by the Christian public with certain funds for the express purpose of providing for the more extensive preaching of the Gopel to our destitute population. We are not merely to give salaries to a number of *men* or even to *ordained men*, or even to *respectable and well educated men*, but we must go further and ask for sufficient evidence that the persons to whom we grant

stipends really know and value the Gospel and
purpose to preach it.'

"That, said the objectors, is going beyond your
province. If the incumbent of a parish selects a
curate and the Bishop examines and approves
him their approbation ought to be enough for you.
You may inquire into the statistics of the case,
you may decide whether or not you will grant aid
to that parish, but as to the curate selected, if the
incumbent and bishop agree on this point we
cannot permit you, a mixed Committee of clergy
and laity sitting in London, to interfere in the
matter."

"But at that rate, said the Committee, if an
incumbent is satisfied with a Tractarian, and such a
nominee can contrive to evade the Bishop's examination, we may be using the Society's money to
propagate deadly error."

"You must leave that to the Bishops, said the
objectors. We cannot do so, said the Committee ;
the public have given us their money upon the
faith of our determination to take care that as far
as we can provide, it shall be expended solely for
the extension of the preaching of the Gospel. If
they find us paying the stipends of Tractarian, or
idle, or ball frequenting curates they will withdraw their confidence and our Society will come
to an end."

"We cannot help that, said the objectors :—if

you persist in interfering with these matters, we
shall set up another Society. And so they did."
(*Churchman's Review*, 1843.)

SPEECH OF REV. DR. HOOK.

The Rev. Dr, Hook, in the course of a speech
delivered on the 6th of February, 1841, gave the
following account of the reasons for the formation
of the Additional Curates Society:—"The Church
Pastoral-Aid Society was formed in the Diocese
of London and in the province of Canterbury, and
I find it recorded that on the 9th of February,
1837, the Rev. Thomas Dale submitted to the
Society the proposal of the Bishop of London,
who acted after consultation with the Archbishop of
Canterbury, which was that the Seventh Regulation
should be expunged and the following substituted, viz. : that applications be received by the
Society for clerical assistance only; that they be
addressed by the incumbent to the Committee,
accompanied with adequate information concerning the character of the individual to be
employed and the amount of service to be performed, but that no grant shall take place until
the proposed object of its appropriation shall
have been communicated by the applicant to the
Bishop of the Diocese. Mr. Dale added that he
was enabled to state that were this alteration made
in the Society's Regulations and were the clergy

allowed their due influence in the Committee,
the countenance of the Bishop of London and of
the Primate, and as a natural consequence of the
whole Episcopal bench, might be confidently expected.

"The Pastoral-Aid Society rejected the proposal. The Lord Archbishop of the Province and
the Lord Bishop of the Diocese condescended to
make an offer to persons who if they were Scriptural Christians were bound to obey them on a
matter relating to the spiritual interests of their
province and of the diocese, and that offer was
rejected; no alternative was left. The rejected
Bishop and the rejected Archbishop, in conjunc-
tion with the other bishops, instituted the Society
for the employment of additional curates, and they
were supported by those who humbly thought
that the Archbishop of Canterbury and the Bishop
of London were more likely to be right and were
more likely to receive God's blessing on their
labours than a combination of individuals, how
ever respectable (and most respectable they were,
though not, I believe, exclusively Churchmen),
who were stretching themselves beyond their line
and were evidently busybodies in other men's
matters."

PRINCIPLE OF "THE VETO" ATTACKED—PAMPHLETS
ON THE SUBJECT.

Complaints began to be current at this time
with respect to the inquiries which the Committee
of the Society made respecting the character and
qualifications of those who were to be supported
by its funds. The Committee, it was alleged,
were guilty of undue interference with the authority of the Church in deciding what applications
they should comply with, and what refuse as
unsatisfactory. The Rev. J. E. N. Molesworth,
D.D., Vicar of Rochdale, attacked the principle of
"the Veto" in a series of pamphlets. During the
years 1840-41 the following publications upon the
controversy appeared:—"*Letter to the Bishop of
Chester upon Certain Symptoms, of Sectarian Designs in the Pastoral-Aid Society, and upon the
Catholic, Comprehensive, and Church Regulations of
the Society for Promoting the Employment of Additional Curates in Populous Parishes,*" by the Rev.
J. E. N. Molesworth, D.D., Vicar of Rochdale.
"*Second Edition of the above, with Observations on
the Answers Attempted.*" "*Letter to the Friends
and Subscribers of the Church Pastoral-Aid Society,
occasioned by a Letter from the Rev. Dr. Molesworth, to the Lord Bishop of Chester, containing
Allegations against the Society,*" by the Rev. *Caleb
Whitefoord.* "*Symptoms of the Dangerous Hands
by which the Insidious Veto of the Pastoral-Aid*

Society may be Wielded, set forth in a Letter to the
Rev. Caleb Whitefoord, on the Fallacies and Un-
worthy Arts used by him and others in Defence of
the Society," by J. E. N. Molesworth, D.D., Vicar of
Rochdale. "Letter to a Member of the Committee
of the Church Pastoral-Aid Society, in Reference to
Certain Animadversions upon that Society recently
published by the Rev. Dr. Molesworth, Vicar of
Rochdale," by the Rev. John Harding, M.A. "Re-
marks on a Letter lately published by Mr. Harding
in Defence of the Principles and Practice of the
Church Pastoral-Aid Society," by the Rev. G. Clayton,
Rector of Warmingham.

The following is an outline of the controversy
upon the question of the Veto of the Committee.
The Rev. Dr. Molesworth, in the course of his
first pamphlet, "*A Letter to the Bishop of Chester*
upon Certain Symptoms of Sectarian Designs, &c.,"
expressed his desire that to the incumbents
should be left the undoubted right of choosing
their own curates, subject to no control but that
of their ecclesiastical superior, the bishop, with
no conditions which interfered with their conscientious views of duty. In his "*Symptoms of*
the Dangerous Hands by which the Insidious Veto
of the Pastoral-Aid Society, &c., &c.," he observed :
—"To prevent misapprehension or misstatement,
I give a brief summary of what I have and what
I have not attempted to establish. I do not ques-

tion the right of the Society to impose its own conditions, but I do question its right having such conditions to be considered or supported as a Church Society. I regard it as a party Society. I do not affirm that these conditions were designed, but I say they are adapted and have been worked to party purposes. I do not charge the whole [illegible] incumbent's right to appoint his own curate, when in practice it retains a veto which can be worked to the subversion of the one and the invasion of the other......It is the incumbent, not the Society, who, according to the order of the Church which the Society professes to respect, is responsible for the choice of his curate, and whom the Society insults by refusing to trust him with that choice, and deceives with the promise of that power which, by its veto, it endeavours to wrest from him......With respect to the Pastoral-Aid Society, I would gladly see its career of good unobstructed, and see its workings as a sister to the Additional Curates Society for the Church."

The Rev. W. Sinclair, in a pamphlet dated 4th February, 1841, entitled "Reasons for supporting the Pastoral-Aid Society," called attention to the fact that "The chief charge alleged against the Society was, that before making a grant it required satisfactory proof to be laid before the Clerical Committee as to the qualifications of the minister to be employed." To this charge Mr. Sinclair offered the following reply:—

The compilers of our Articles and Homilies . . . declared in the XXVIth Article . . . that "*in the visible Church the evil will be ever mingled with the good, and sometimes the evil have chief authority in the ministration of the Word and sacraments.*" And they have strengthened this position by expressly declaring in the Homilies that *" sincere preachers ever were and ever shall be few in respect to the multitude to be taught, for our Saviour Christ saith the harvest is plentiful but the workmen be but few, which hath been hitherto continually true and will be to the world's end."* Now, the supporters of the Pastoral-Aid Society cannot desire a more secure shelter from the charge of unmeet severity than is here afforded them by the Fathers of the Reformation when they affirm that the clergy of any Church, and of our own among them, are a mingled body where the faithful and the unfaithful are mixed together. . . . Are there none of our clergy who, instead of knowing nothing among their people save Jesus Christ and Him crucified, would exercise reserve in communicating to them the doctrine of the Atonement? And is it to be wondered at that the Society under such circumstances should seek by every legitimate means to be satisfied as to the fitness of the individual proposed? But this is done, it is alleged, in an irregular and uncanonical manner. No Society composed of private individuals has a right " to send forth labourers into the vineyard " or to test the qualifications of the clergy. Now, as to the first part of this charge, I must reiterate the often-repeated fact that the Society does not send forth the labourers : it only provides the salary ; the incumbent alone must find the man. And as to the test of qualification, I have an equally satisfactory reply. . . . The venerable " Society for the Propagation of the Gospel in Foreign Parts " is an unquestionable Church Society : no one presumes to dispute its claim to that title. Let me call attention to the XVIIth Rule of this Society.

XVII. *That no missionary be employed until the fullest inquiry has been made into his fitness and efficiency, and that all persons applying for Missions shall produce testimonials, signed by three beneficed clergymen, and countersigned by the bishop of the diocese in which those clergymen are beneficed.*

The Society does not therefore require *anything* on this subject but what its predecessor required before it. If the Propagation Society, with its XVIIth Rule unrepealed, is a Church Society, then the Pastoral-Aid Society may put in as valid a claim. The Rev. J. Harding, Rector of St. Anne's, Blackfriars, London, in his " *Letter to a Member of the Committee of the Church Pastoral-Aid Society,*" which appeared in 1841, observed : " I am free to confess that among the objectors to our Society on the ground of its claim to be satisfied of the qualification of parties nominated to occupy its grants, there were some whose station in the Church and whose personal character so far weighed with me, that, although when I first joined the Society I did so from a persuasion that

it was strictly in accordance with Church of
England principles, I was led to pause for the
purpose of reconsidering our position, and inquiring honestly and seriously, are we, or are we
not, contravening any established order of the
Church which we are bound to obey? The result
of that reconsideration of the question has been
just the opposite to Dr. Molesworth's affirmation.
. . . . When I look at the exceeding care which
the Church in her Canons and Ordination Service
prescribes in investigating the character and qualifications of every person before he be admitted to
a spiritual charge, I must own that I think our
course much more in accordance with her spirit
than in contravention of it."

The following extract from the " Churchman's
Review " for 1841, p. 232, fairly exhibits the state
of the case :—" An incumbent needs a curate, and
having no sufficient means to provide one at his
own charge, he applies to the Church Pastoral-
Aid Society for assistance, and obtains a grant. It
is then left to him to select his assistant, but the
Society requires to be informed of the name,
qualifications, and character of the person selected,
and expects that its Clerical Committee shall be
satisfied on these points by testimony from competent referees before the bishop is applied to for
his licence.

" Two kinds of misrepresentations are frequently

SKETCH OF ITS ORIGIN AND PROGRESS.

met with as to these proceedings. It is sometimes said that the Society rejects a candidate
after the Bishop has approved him, thus setting
its judgment above that of the Diocesan. The
fact, however, is, that the Society is most desirous
of avoiding any such apparent disrespect, and
therefore in all cases warns incumbents *not* to
offer their candidates to the diocesan *until* the
Committee and themselves shall have agreed as
to their fitness and qualifications. In the case of
the Church Pastoral-Aid Society, the scrutiny is
strictly confined to a Committee of twelve clergymen, whose inquiries are conducted in the most
delicate and considerate manner.

" The Church Pastoral-Aid Society, when it is to
furnish the stipend of a curate, requires some-
thing more than the mere customary testimonials.
It interposes not in the selection; it suggests
nothing, proposes nothing, leaves the incumbent
to his own free volition in this matter; but if he
be so careless, or so hasty, as to nominate a curate
of whom no one will frankly, and in a private
letter of his own, declare that he is a zealous and
devoted man, the Society remembers that it is
charged with an important trust, that its funds are
painfully collected in small sums from the
middling, and even the poorer classes, and it
replies through its Clerical Committee that it
cannot thus misappropriate the funds committed
to its charge."

The following extract from the original pro-
spectus of the Society has an important bearing
on this question :—" Let no one imagine that the
establishment of the Society is proposed with the
remotest design of infringing on the operations
of others which are employed for the benefit of
England in connection with the Church, or of
prosecuting its work in opposition to the Ecclesiastical authorities. On the contrary, its agency
will come in to the assistance of every other
Church Society."

SOME TESTIMONIES OF CLERGY REGARDING LAY AGENCY.

The Rev. J. N. Pearson, in preaching before
the Society in 1837, observed, " The Society does
not refuse to sanction the engagement of lay-
agents and to assign them a stipend. When the
need of spiritual help is urgent, and that of the
clergyman not to be obtained, it sees nothing in
the Word of God, nothing in Ecclesiastical law,
nothing in the measure itself, when tried by
reason and experience, to preclude it from calling
into the service of the Church men not in holy
orders. Every lay-agent is under a solemn stipu-
lation to abstain from functions that are purely
spiritual. He is selected by the incumbent whom
he is paid to assist, is placed absolutely under his
control, and is removable at his discretion. The

Society takes no further part in the affair than first to ascertain the urgency of the case, then the qualifications of the nominee, and afterwards to pay his salary.

The Bishop of Chester, in his sermon before the Society in 1838, thus referred to the principle of lay-agency:—" I think it no disparagement to the Society that it supplies the salary of a number of lay-assistants. If no lay-assistant may receive a salary, no lay-assistant may be employed. The same principle which forbids his salary must refuse his aid. In many cases the expediency may be questioned—of that let the incumbents judge ; but for the legality I must earnestly contend, for if our clergy in their spiritual labours are to receive no aid or co-operation except from clergy like themselves, they must sink under an intolerable burthen, or their people ' perish for lack of knowledge.' Still, let me not be mistaken, as if I would be the author of confusion. The minister has his distinct duty, the duty to which he is called, to which he is set apart as the ordained dispenser of God's Word and Sacraments, as minister of the congregation in which he is appointed to serve. . . . I hold it to be no disparagement to the Society that it admits of lay assistance, that it so far admits the principle as to allow the incumbent of a parish, if he sees fit, to employ a layman. . . . Whether curate or lay assistant, the incumbent is the responsible employer; the Society furnishes but the salary."

Archdeacon Shirley affirmed in a speech, delivered in 1844, "It is, I think, sufficiently clear that in the early Church the Apostles themselves were 'helped much in the Lord' by laymen. All our missionary societies employ unordained catechists to aid the ministerial work. And in this great city of London necessity of the case has forced upon the Church the employment of lay assistants.* You dared to send men to work in co-operation with the ministers of the Church just as in Apostolic days laymen were 'thrust out' into the vineyard in the time of the persecution that arose about Stephen, to do the Lord's work. You have Apostolical authority, therefore, and these men, though laymen, may claim some title, at least, to have Apostolical succession."

The Rev. J. B. Owen, of Bilston, in a speech delivered in 1844, thus stated the argument for lay agency: "I should be prepared to discuss the propriety of employing lay agency, and first upon Scriptural grounds. It would be difficult to prove the orders of Apollos, who is described as 'an eloquent man,' like many of the lay agents, and

* In allusion to the "Association for providing Scripture Readers in connection with the Church of England."

' mighty in the Scriptures,' instructed in the way of the Lord, fervent in spirit, and who mightily convinced the Jews, and that publicly, showing by the Scriptures that Jesus is the Christ. It would be difficult to prove the orders of Priscilla and Aquila. . . . Had the old word catechist been kept up, opponents might have been silenced by showing that Origen was associated with St. Mark, the first Bishop of Alexandria, as a catechist. I defend lay agency on the ground that it is one great practical means of showing an example to the laity of co-operating with the clergy. . . . Lay agency was the only existing opportunity in connection with the Church of affording a preliminary period of discipline to the candidate for holy orders."

The Rev. E. Bickersteth, in a speech in 1845, on the same subject, remarked: " I feel attached to the Society because it maintains lay teachers of sound principles. I feel this to be an important principle, because I see it distinctly in the Word of God ; and sure I am that those who talk of Apostolic Churches and the Fathers need not object, for if they read they will find that lay teachers were occasionally called upon even by the bishop 'to instruct the congregation. In the earliest times of the Church lay teaching formed a part of the primitive plan of the Church, under the direction of the ministers of the Word."

REV. JOHN DAVIES'S MISSION TO BOATMEN.

Amongst the Occasional Papers issued at this
time, No. VI., for January, 1839, may be specially
noted. It stated that thirty-five new associations
had been formed since July, 1838, and also contained interesting memoranda with regard to work
among the Canal and River Boatmen of the
Severn, and the Worcester and Birmingham Canal.
The Rev. John Davies, styled the "Apostle of
the Watermen," was distinguished for his labours
on behalf of the boatmen on our rivers and canals,
of which Runcorn, in Cheshire, was for a season
the central point. This town was especially
adapted for the purpose of being a missionary
port to watermen, inasmuch as three great chan-
nels of inland communication met there, viz.:
the Bridgwater Canal, the Mersey, and Irwell, as
well as the Weaver Navigation. It was calculated
at this time that there were about 120 canals in
the United Kingdom, extending nearly 3,000
miles. The men employed on these canals and
on our navigable rivers, with their families, gave
a population of nearly 10,000 souls.

The number of boatmen, including their wives
and children, frequenting the navigations connected with Worcester, it was estimated amounted
to about 4,000, not including coalheavers. Between January, 1836, and December, 1846, it
appeared that 302 boatmen were committed to

Worcester Gaol alone; *of this number only one could read and write well.* The Rev. John Davies entered upon his labours at Runcorn in September, 1888. The Society materially assisted him in this work. Mr. Davies stated, in the course of a letter to the Bishop of Chester, dated 26th March, 1839, that he " trusted ere long to have another clergyman appointed for the watermen. There was one clergyman at Manchester, paid by the Church Pastoral-Aid Society, and three clergy he hoped would soon be at work." Mr. Davies's plan for a floating watermen's church, commenced in 1840, was carried out in 1842. The Bishop of Chester, when the vessel was licensed, expressed a wish that Mr. Davies should occasionally exchange duty with the chaplain.

During his stay at Runcorn, Mr. Davies laid the foundation-stones of three churches (Trinity Church being completed in 1838) on the Weaver Navigation, one at Weston Point, the other inland, with all those external accompaniments which tend so much to the social benefit of the people. The complete cessation of Sunday traffic also was, through the Divine blessing, accomplished on several canals, which was continued on the Weaver Navigation entirely, and in others partially.

The " Occasional Paper" for March, 1839, was addressed more particularly to the proprietors of railroads, canals, mines, &c.; and enclosed con-

tents of a letter, subscribed "R. F. D. S.," referring especially to the state of canal boatmen and
colliers, and enclosing a donation, with hopes that
it might be used as the commencement of a fund
to be appropriated peculiarly to the instruction of
the above-mentioned class. The Committee also
announced in this paper that since January, 1839,
the Bishops of Bath and Wells and of Sodor and
Man had become Vice-Presidents.

The "Occasional Paper" for December, 1839,
contained extracts from the Minutes of the Sub-
Committee within one month, viz.: from 22nd
of October to 19th November, showing the cases
and correspondence and the urgency of the claims
on the funds of the Society. Among the cases
in this Paper were two from the disturbed districts
in Wales to which the Committee directed special
attention.

"SYNOPSIS" OF THE SOCIETY.

In view of the misunderstanding arising from
the erroneous statements so frequently circulated
respecting the Society, the Committee published
in this Paper the following "Synopsis of the
Society" :—

OBJECT.—The salvation of souls, with a single
eye to the glory of God, and in humble depend-
ence on His blessing, by granting aid towards
maintaining faithful and devoted men to assist the
incumbents of parishes in their pastoral charge.

PRINCIPLES.—That in a Christian land a Church established should adequately provide for the spiritual instruction of all the people, and that it is part of the duty of a Christian Legislature to furnish the Church with means for this end, but that if the Legislature should fail of this duty, then, rather than souls should perish, Christian men must join together to supply the deficiency and make the Church as effective as it is in their power to do.

PLAN.—The Church Pastoral-Aid Society strictly regards the wants of the Church on the one hand and the order of the Church on the other. It would make the Church efficient; it would carry the Gospel by means of the Church to every man's door, but it never obtrudes its aid; the incumbent must apply for aid or sanction the application, and until this is done, the Society cannot move. When aid is sought and granted, the parochial minister must say how it is employed; he must nominate the persons to be employed; he must engage them as well as superintend and entirely control them; all that the Society does is to provide for their remuneration, and while doing so to ask satisfactory proof of their qualifications.

CHURCH BUILDING.

It was proposed, at the date of its institution, that the Society should afford aid in the erection

E

of buildings. The effect of the Church Building
Act of 1818 (the first public and general Act of
the kind), when Parliament granted 1,000,000*l.*
towards the erection of additional churches in
populous districts, was referred to in the early
publications of the Society. It was thought desirable that the Society's aid in this respect should
not be limited to very populous districts only,
but should be likewise extended to the country
districts, many of which exhibited some of the
strongest possible claims on Christian piety.
Villages and hamlets were to be found without
church or school, their inhabitants, by reason of
their distant and secluded situation, almost cut
off from pastoral supervision, and living in
deplorable ignorance of Christian faith and duty.

On behalf of such spots applications were frequently made to the Committee, and it was urged
that places of worship might be provided for them,
but the difficulty was to raise, at least for some
few years, the smallest stipend suitable for a resident minister. This deficiency the Pastoral-Aid
Society was solicited, either in whole or in part,
to supply. And the Committee stated that they
felt much satisfaction in reporting that the
aid requested having been given, churches and
chapels which without such help would not have
been attempted were rising, clergymen were
stationed in those hitherto neglected hamlets,

congregations were gathering, and most happy consequences, temporal and spiritual, resulting.

The Fifth Annual Meeting of the Society was held in the great room, Exeter Hall, on Tuesday, the 12th of May, 1840, Lord Ashley in the chair. The speakers were the Bishops of Chester, Lichfield, Norwich, and Ripon; the Revs. J. Furnivall, J. B. Marsden, Chancellor Raikes, W. Sinclair, H. Stowell, and E. Tottenham,

In the eighth Occasional Paper, published in November, 1840, the Committee called the particular attention of the friends and supporters of the Church Pastoral-Aid Society to the fact that, in consequence of the increased expenditure, they felt they could not comply with any fresh applications, and accordingly, at a meeting of the General Committee, it was resolved—" That in the present state of the Society's funds, it is expedient to inform the applicants for aid that the Committee regret they are compelled to forbear entering into the consideration of any new cases until the result of an earnest appeal for increased contributions in support of the Society's objects has transpired." This Occasional Paper contained a map.

The next Occasional Paper appeared in January, 1841. Owing to a want of funds on the one hand, and mistaken representations on the other, the Committee published a Table showing the extent of the Society's operations, and the re-

sults of aid at that time. The charge on
the Society greatly exceeded the income, and
5,000*l.* of the Reserve Fund had to be
withdrawn, and the Committee felt themselves
bound to renew the Resolution proposed in
November, 1840.

ERROR RESPECTING NOMINATIONS.

They also explained the course pursued by
them in respect of nominations, as it had
been erroneously stated that the nominees were
examined by, and their testimonials submitted
to a lay Committee. Such was never the case.
An incumbent, before his case was taken into
consideration, had the " Circular to Applicants
for Aid " forwarded to him, and was also furnished
with copies of Regulations II., III., and VIII., in
*which he was distinctly advised of the course required
and pursued in regard to nominations.*

SIXTH ANNIVERSARY.

The Sixth Annual Meeting was held in the
large room, Exeter Hall, on the 11th of May,
1841, Lord Ashley in the chair. The speakers
were the Bishops of Chester, Lichfield, and
Winchester; the Revs. C. J. Goodhart, H.
McNeile, and others. The Annual Sermon was
preached in St. Dunstan's Church, Fleet Street,
London, by the Rev. J. Harding, Rector of St.

Ann's, Blackfriars, London, on the text, Romans i., part of 16th verse.

The Report announced that the Bishop of Chichester had added his name to the list of Vice-Patrons in the room of his lamented predecessor in that see; also that the Right Hon. Lord Cal-thorpe, the Regius Professor of Divinity at Oxford, the Right Hon. H. Goulburn, M.P., the Right Hon. Sir George Rose, M.P., the Hon. Arthur Kinnaird, and the Hon. Baron Gurney, had become Vice-Presidents of the Society; that nearly 1,700 clergymen were now members of the Society, the list of clerical members having been increased by the addition of upwards of 270 names. Several clergymen in various parts of the country had consented to act as corresponding members of the Society.

CLASSIFICATION OF GRANTS.

The grants at this time were classed under the following heads:—

1. For curates, to assist incumbents in populous places.

2. For curates, to have charge of distant hamlets and townships where a new population has sprung up and Church ordinances had been for the most part unknown.

3. To retain the services of incumbents in populous and ill-endowed districts which they would otherwise be compelled to quit.

4. For chaplains, for the spiritual instruction of the labourers on several lines of railway now in formation; and for clergymen, to have special charge of watermen on canals, &c.

5. For lay assistants, acting under the direction of the incumbents simply as district visitors, Scripture-readers, tract distributors, but by no means as public instructors and teachers.

6. To these may be added a few grants, under peculiar circumstances, towards the purchase or fitting-up of chapels and school rooms for Divine service.

PROPOSAL TO APPOINT AN ASSOCIATION SECRETARY.

The Committee felt it incumbent on them to direct their special attention to the formation of Auxiliary Associations throughout the country, regarding them as the principal means by which the funds of the Society were to be regularly sustained and augmented. For the better promotion of this important object, they deemed it expedient that, in addition to the Travelling Secretary, a Secretary should be appointed, to be called the "Association Secretary," whose peculiar province it should be to superintend the Association Department, to open correspondence with the clergy throughout the country respecting the formation of his Auxiliaries, and by every other means in his power to extend the influence and pecuniary resources of the Society.

SEVENTH ANNIVERSARY.

The Seventh Annual Meeting was held in the large room, Exeter Hall, on the 10th of May, 1842, Lord Ashley in the chair. The speakers were the Bishops of Llandaff and Norwich, the Earl of Harrowby, K.G., the Revs. J. Harding, H. Raikes, H. Stowell, and the Hon. M. Villiers. The Annual Sermon was preached in St. Dunstan's Church, Fleet Street, London, by the Rev. Henry Raikes, M.A., Chancellor of the Diocese of Chester, upon the text St. Matt. ix. 38.

The Committee observed in the "Occasional Paper" for January, 1842, that during the six years of the Society's existence it had provided for the services of at least 250 additional clergymen.

A principal ground on which the Society rested its claims to the support of the Christian public was the insufficiency of pecuniary means possessed by many of the incumbents of our Church. The Committee invited special attention to the fact that of the 10,500 benefices in England and Wales, there were 3,528 whose income was below 150*l.* per annum. And many of these benefices had a disproportionately large population annexed to them.

The average income of the incumbents aided by the Society was about 160*l.* per annum, while the average population was upwards of 7,000. One great object of the Society, it was stated, was to enable incumbents with such limited means to enjoy the same advantages, in reference to clerical aid, which their brethren, who were more blessed in a temporal point of view, had the means of procuring from their own ecclesiastical resources.

The grants of the Society in January, 1842, were 255 for clergymen, 35 for lay assistants, and 26 for miscellaneous purposes; of these 55 grants were not in operation. The annual payments of the Society were 22,000*l.* Its actual liabilities (as the grants above-mentioned might at any time become operative) were 26,000*l.*; whereas it was to be feared that the income of the Society for that year would fall short of that of 1841, which was 19,665*l.* It was also to be observed that the Society had been compelled to employ nearly the whole of its Reserve Fund.

The Committee, in adverting to the opposition which had been undeservedly raised against the Society by misrepresentations respecting its objects and principles, and to the fact that its character and appellation of a Church Society had been called in question, referred to the admirable letter of the Bishop of Llandaff and to the speeches of the Bishops of Winchester, Chester, and Lichfield, which were read and delivered at the last Anniversary.

EIGHTH ANNIVERSARY.

The Eighth Anniversary Meeting was held in the large room, Exeter Hall, on Tuesday, the 9th of May, 1843, Lord Ashley in the chair. The speakers were the Bishops of Chester, Llandaff, and Norwich, Archdeacon Shirley, the Revs. E. Bickersteth, J. Scholefield, H. Stowell, and the Hon. M. Villiers. The Annual Sermon was preached in St. Dunstan's Church, Fleet Street, London, by the Rev. James Scholefield, M.A., Regius Professor of Greek in the University of Cambridge, from the words of the Gospel of St. Matthew ix. 35—38.

The " Occasional Paper " (No. XII.) for March, 1843, contained a complete tabulated list of the Society's grants arranged under the several dioceses.

SOCIETY'S BALANCE AT END OF YEAR.

The Committee, in the same Paper, called attention to the fact that the expenditure of the Society exceeded the income, and had done so for the last three years, at the rate of 2,000l. per annum, and that the deficiency had hitherto been supplied from the balance which accumulated during the early years of the Society's operations. This balance had already been reduced further than was consistent with safety. It might be asked what necessity was there for any balance at the end of the year? This question was best answered by the statement of a fact. On the 1st of April, 1842, the balance in hand amounted to 6,500*l.* ; it was reduced to 2,375*l.* in August, and *the whole amount* was required to meet the quarterly stipends due in November ; and on the 14th of March the balance in hand only amounted to 1,100*l.* ; this arose from the greater part of the income being received in the latter half of the year. Thus, judging from experience, it was obvious that it was *absolutely necessary to have a balance of at least* 6,000*l.* at the commencement of the year to enable the Committee to meet its engagements.

It was moreover intimated that unless a decided increase took place in the Society's income, it would be necessary to effect an immediate reduction of grants to the extent of 2,000*l.* per annum.

The alternatives before the Committee were, of immediately giving up grants to the amount of 2,500*l.*, or of borrowing at the November quarter between 2,000*l.* and 3,000*l.* With sincere thankfulness, the Committee reported in the Occasional Paper for December, 1843, that they had not been compelled to adopt either alternative. The grants, except in one or two instances, had been continued, the quarterly payments had been made, and a small balance still remained towards the next quarter's expenditure. Indeed, the Committee, encouraged by the liberality of their friends, had ventured to make fifteen fresh grants, thirteen for curates and two for lay assistants.

SKETCH OF ITS ORIGIN AND PROGRESS.

CAUSES OF INCREASE OF INCOME.

This increase of income was, under the Divine blessing, to be attributed to several causes :—1. To the impression produced by a letter from the President of the Society addressed to the nobility and gentry of the metropolis, accompanying a statement of numerous applications for aid. 2. To the increased support from branch societies and associations, many of which had doubled their former amount of contributions; and to a great addition in the list of life and yearly subscribers. 3. To the formation of several new associations, viz.—Rugby, under the patronage of the Bishop of Worcester ; Watton and Herts Auxiliary, promoted by the Rev. Edward Bickersteth, and presided over by Abel Smith, Esq., M.P. ; Tonbridge, and its vicinity—President, the Rev. Sir Charles Hardinge; Oldham, under the patronage of the Bishop of Chester ; Hampstead—President, Captain Sir W. E. Parry, R.N.; also Litcham, Axminster, and Burton Coggles; and lastly from the statements of the religious destitution of the country, especially in the manufacturing districts, made by Sir Robert Peel and Lord Ashley in bringing forward their measures for Church extension and for the education of the poor.

NINTH ANNIVERSARY.

The Ninth Annual Meeting was held in the large room, Exeter Hall, on Tuesday, 7th of May, 1844, the Hon. Captain Waldegrave, R.N., in the chair. The speakers were the Earl of Chichester, Archdeacon Shirley, the Revs. Edward Auriol, W. W. Champneys, J. Harding, J. B. Owen, and D. Wilson, and Mr. J. Labouchere (Treasurer of the Society). The annual sermon was preached in St. Dunstan's Church, Fleet-street, London, on Monday, May 6th, 1844, by the Ven. Archdeacon Shirley, M.A., from the words of the Gospel St. Luke v. 7.

The Annual Report stated that the increase in the number of associations, and also in the remittances from nearly all of them, was greatly to be attributed to the efforts which had been made by the two Association Secretaries. It was quite beyond their power to visit all the places required, much less to seek for new friends and supporters in those parts of the country where the Society was little known. The Committee had, therefore, after much careful consideration, determined to appoint a third clergyman to assist in that work.

TENTH ANNIVERSARY.

The Tenth Annual Meeting was held in the Freemasons' Hall, Great Queen Street, London, on Thursday, the 8th of May, 1845, Lord Ashley in the chair. The speakers were the Revs. Edward Bickersteth, F. Close, Dr. Marsh, Chancellor Raikes, Hugh Stowell, E. Tottenham, Hon. M. Villiers, and the Hon. Captain Waldegrave, R.N., C.B.

"PEEL" DISTRICTS.

The Committee, in the Occasional Paper No. XIV., for December, 1844, called special attention to an erroneous impression existing with respect to the provision effected under the recent Act of Sir Robert Peel, which in no way superseded the necessity for the operations of the Church Pastoral-Aid Society. The object of the Act was to subdivide populous and extensive parishes into manageable districts, and the Committee had good authority for stating that the applications from various parts of the country had been far greater in number than the Commissioners would be able to grant. The total number of districts to be formed would be limited to 200; of this number about one-third had been completed, and had now clergymen appointed to them. But although there were upon the list of the Society's existing grants no less than ninety-six parishes or districts, with populations varying from 8,000 to 30,000 souls, thirteen only of these had received assistance from the operation of that Act, and even in these cases the Society had not been relieved of its grants, for the amount of population left under the charge of these incumbents after the assignment of the districts had. been larger than they could by any possibility superintend; in some cases the amount had been above 10,000, and in no case less than 5,000 or 6,000: consequently, although these parishes at large had been greatly benefited, the incumbents still needed the assistance of fellow-labourers as before; and the grants, with only one exception, had been continued. Besides this, in some cases the new districts were so large, having populations of from 5,000 to 8,000, that the ministers appointed to those very districts had applied to the Society for assistance. . . . . If twice the number of districts were endowed, and the number of the Society's grants doubled, and diligent and devoted men of God at work upon them all, there would even then be many a district unprovided for, and multitudes in this Christian land beyond the reach of the pastor's visits and exhortation.

ELEVENTH ANNIVERSARY.

The Eleventh Annual Meeting was held in the large room, Exeter Hall, on Tuesday, the 12th of May, 1846, Lord Ashley in the chair. The speakers were the Bishops of Chester, Llandaff, Norwich, and Winchester, the Revs. F. Ould, W. Pollock, W. Sinclair, Hugh Stowell, and the Hon. M. Villiers. The sermon was preached in

St. Dunstan's Church, Fleet Street, London, on
Monday, 11th of May, 1846, by the Rev. John
Hambleton, M.A., minister of the Chapel of Ease,
Islington, London, upon the text 1 Cor. xvi. 9.

The Committee announced, with regret, the
decease of the Bishop of Bath and Wells—" from
this venerable Prelate the Society had uniformly
received cordial countenance and support,"—and of
the Rev. E. F. Champneys, Secretary of the
Society.   The Committee also stated that the
Bishops of Oxford and of Calcutta, and the Earl
of Effingham, had accepted the office of Vice-
Patrons.

The vacancy caused by the death of Mr. Champneys was supplied by the appointment of the Rev.
Charles Clayton, M.A., one of the Senior Fellows
of Caius College, Cambridge.

The Committee hoped shortly to be able to
elect an Association Secretary for the Southern
District, in the place of the Rev. D. Cooke, of
whose services the Society had been deprived
by his appointment to the office of Secretary of
the Church of England Society for Educating
the Poor in Newfoundland and the Colonies.

" SCOTT " LEGACY.

The Committee recorded a munificent legacy
from the late John Scott, of Park Lane, Piccadilly,
and formerly of New Broad Street, London.   A

sum had already been paid, amounting to 7,321*l.*, and a further sum would accrue at a period yet future.

The Committee published the following statement, exhibiting the receipts and disbursements of the Society for each year of the first decade of the Society's existence :—

INCOME AND EXPENDITURE OF THE CHURCH PASTORAL-AID SOCIETY, 1836 TO 1845.

INCOME			EXPENDITURE								
—	—		Grants			Management			Total		
	£	*s.*	*d.*	£	*s.*	*d.*	£	*s.*	*d.*	£	*s.*	*d.*
1836-7	7,363	11	0	748	18	1	855	12	0	1,604	10	1
1837-8	8,113	15	11	3,298	16	4	1,505	15	5	4,804	11	9
1838-9	10,423	4	5	7,733	14	8	1,993	11	2	9,727	5	10
1839-40	17,562	19	11	11,475	9	11	2,600	4	8	14,075	14	7
1840-1	19,665	16	5	18,857	14	1	2,911	19	7	21,769	13	8
1841-2	18,880	15	2	18,960	11	7	3,019	19	7	21,980	11	2
1842-3	17,562	19	11	17,362	9	8	2,846	18	2	20,209	7	10
1843-4	21,828	5	6	16,504	17	2	2,962	15	3	19,467	12	5
1844-5	20,426	12	10	16,651	2	3	2,412	8	2	19,063	10	5
1845-6	22,505	17	7	18,895	3	10	2,811	11	5	21,706	15	3

An analysis of the above tabular statement showed a progressive advance in the funds of the Society, from an average amount of 8,633*l.* for the first three years, to 18,703*l.* for the second, and to 19,939*l.* for the third like periods; while

the income of the tenth year—viz., 22,505*l*. 17*s*. 7*d*.
—had reached an amount unequalled in any year
preceding.

"PEEL" DISTRICTS.

The Committee observed that, so far from
the operations of the Ecclesiastical Commissioners, and those under the Act of Sir Robert
Peel, relative to the subdivision of large parishes,
having rendered the work of the Society less
necessary, it was a noteworthy fact that, of those
districts which had been thus formed and endowed,
there were no fewer than seventy-seven deriving
aid from the Society.

MISSION TO BOATMEN, &c.

The Society's work of supporting clergymen to
labour amongst Boatmen, Railway Labourers, and
Bargemen, commenced in this year, with a grant
to a chaplain in the north of England, having
under his charge 1,600 railway labourers; also
to the vicar of a parish containing 7,000 souls
for the maintenance of services for Bargemen in
the Floating Chapel.

RESOLUTIONS REGARDING "SCOTT" LEGACY.

The Committee, in a Supplement to the Report,
called the special attention of their friends to the
following Resolutions, passed at a Special Meeting

F

on the 18th June, 1846, with reference to the bequest of the late John Scott:—

1. Resolved—That in the opinion of this Committee, the sentiments expressed in the will of the late Mr. Scott will be best responded to by the application of a portion of his munificent legacy to the immediate extension of the sphere of the Society's operations.

2. Resolved—That, accordingly, a portion of the legacy, amounting to 2,000*l*, be forthwith placed to the account of the income of the current year, for the purpose of enabling the Committee to make twenty new grants, to be called the *Scott* grants.

3. Resolved—That the remaining 5,321*l*. be forthwith invested in Government Long Annuities, expiring January, 1860, so as to ensure an annual income of about 520*l*. for fourteen years.

4. Resolved—That in the opinion of the Committee the proposed additional grants call for increased exertion on the part of the friends of the Society, in order to render this extension of its operations permanent without breaking in on the proposed investment.

CORRESPONDENCE WITH BISHOP OF WINCHESTER.

Correspondence was held with the Bishop of Winchester, who requested the co-operation of the, Society in carrying into execution important

designs for alleviating the spiritual destitution of
the population of Southwark. The Committee,
in confident expectation of increased support,
pledged themselves to make grants to the amount
of 500l. towards maintaining additional clergymen
to take the pastoral oversight of new districts to
be formed there. They also expressed their
willingness to afford aid to a greater extent, if
needed, and if the funds of the Society would
admit.

TWELFTH ANNIVERSARY.

The Twelfth Annual Meeting was held in the
large room, Exeter Hall, on Tuesday, May 11th,
1847, Lord Ashley in the chair. The speakers
were the Bishops of Winchester, Chester, and
Oxford, the Revs. E. Bickersteth, J. W. Brooks,
R. Burgess, Dr. McNeile, and Mr. John Labouchere, Treasurer of the Society. The sermon
was preached by the Rev. Hugh McNeile, D.D.,
Honorary Canon of Chester and minister of St.
Jude's, Liverpool, upon the text Eph. ii. 10.

The Report stated that the Earl Denbigh, the
Earl Waldegrave, and the Bishop of Melbourne
had accepted the office of Vice-Patrons and that
Lord Teignmouth had become a Vice-President.

ASSOCIATION SECRETARIES—REARRANGEMENT OF DISTRICTS.

With regard to Association proceedings the

Committee stated that a fresh arrangement of the districts to be visited by the Association Secretaries had been made as follows :—*Northern*, under the care of the Rev. A. P. Irwine; *Midland*, under the Rev. J. Lees ; *South-Western*, under the Rev. J. G. Kelly ; *South-Eastern*, under the Rev. J. N. Green Armytage. The Rev. A. Wyndham Jones, of Loughor, near Swansea, took charge of the counties of Carmarthen, Glamorgan, and Pembroke.

LARGE NUMBER OF NEW GRANTS.

It was remarked this year that never before had there been so large a number of grants upon the Society's books or so many of them in operation. During the year 119 new grants were made.

Of these new grants two were for chaplains to take the oversight of the navigators and labourers on the Wrexham and North Staffordshire Railways, and two for lay assistants for the benefit of the men employed in the construction of the lines near Reading and Stamford. Eight grants, amounting to 660*l.*, were made to clergymen appointed to new districts, ultimately to be endowed by the Ecclesiastical Commissioners; and eleven, amounting to 1,020*l.*, were for curates to have special charge of districts intended to be formed into district parishes, as soon as endowments from pri-

vate and other sources could be obtained. Seven
grants amounting to 157*l.* were made towards the
fitting up of schoolrooms to be licensed for the
celebration of Divine service in populous and poor
districts. The remaining grants were for 52
curates and 37 lay assistants.

"THE SCOTT GRANTS."

Special reference was made in the Occasional
Paper, No. XVIII., for October, 1846, to "The
Scott Grants." The Committee had stated in
June that it was their intention to appropriate
2,000*l.* of Mr. Scott's legacy to the income of the
current year with the view of making about 20
new grants. The object of the Committee in
applying to immediate use so large a portion of
the legacy, and in purchasing Long Annuities
with the residue, was to avail themselves of so
favourable an opportunity of *permanently enlarg-
ing* the sphere of the Society's labours, under the
full assurance that as the investment would produce only 518*l.* per annum for fourteen years the
members of the Church would raise the 1,482*l.*
required to make up the 2,000*l.*, the amount
necessary to keep the "Scott Grants" in existence.

APPOINTMENT OF ADDITIONAL ASSOCIATION SECRETARY.

To provide for the larger wants of the Society,

and to promote the more efficient superintendence
of the various Associations throughout the country,
the Committee appointed an additional Association Secretary; and they reported that they had
secured the services of the Rev. J. N. Green
Armytage, to act in the South-Eastern district,
in the place of the Rev. D. Cooke; and the Rev.
J. G. Kelly, to take charge of the Society's
interests in the South-Western counties.

THIRTEENTH ANNIVERSARY.

The Thirteenth Annual Meeting was held in the
large room, Exeter Hall, on Tuesday, the 9th of
May, 1848, Lord Ashley in the Chair. The
speakers were the Bishops of Manchester and
Norwich; the Revs. E. Auriol, J. Burnet, LL.D.,
J. Harding, Hon. B. W. Noel, T. Nolan, E. B.
Squire, and Hugh Stowell. The sermon was
preached in St. Dunstan's Church, Fleet Street,
London, on Monday, May 8th, 1848, by the
Rev. John Burnet, LL.D., Vicar of Bradford,
Yorkshire.

With regard to patronage, the Report stated
that the Archbishop of Canterbury, who while
Bishop of Chester was one of the earliest and
most strenuous of the Society's supporters, had
kindly intimated his readiness, in his new and
elevated position, to do all in his power to promote the Society's efficiency.

ADDRESS PRESENTED TO ARCHBISHOP OF CAN-
TERBURY.

The following address was presented to his
Grace on the 6th of April, 1848 :—

" *To the Most Rev. Father in God, John Bird, by Divine
Providence Lord Archbishop of Canterbury, Primate of All
England and Metropolitan.*

" May it please your Grace,—

" The Committee of the Church Pastoral-Aid
Society beg the favour of being allowed to tender to you
the expression of their feelings, on the event of your
Grace's appointment, in the providence of God, to that
high office in which they have now the happiness of
addressing you.

" They indulge the belief, that, in thus approaching
your Grace, it will not be thought that they are presum-
ing too much on the kindness and attention which the
conductors of this Society have always experienced at
your hands : rather they must plead the recollection of
the past as that which enforces from them some tribute of
mingled veneration and gratitude on the present occasion
—a tribute in which they are sure that they do but faintly
echo the sentiments of all the members of the Society at
large. It never can be forgotten by any who have watched
with interest the progress of this Institution, since its
foundation twelve years ago, that it was to the patronage
and counsel which its originators received from you they
were pre-eminently indebted for the success which, under
the Divine favour, attended their endeavours for the service of their Church and the welfare of their land ; neither
can those who have been engaged from year to year in
the details of the management of the Society, ever be

insensible to the value of that wise advice and unabating
support which, on every occasion, they have been per-
mitted to ask and to receive from you.

" Your Grace will therefore bear with the Committee
in soliciting your acceptance from them of this assurance
of their most respectful attachment to your person, their
grateful remembrance of your past kindnesses, their
devout thanksgivings to Almighty God on your recent
elevation, and their fervent prayer that your Grace may
long be spared in the Primacy of their beloved Church
to sustain with increasing honour and comfort the
character, which they have ever delighted to recognize
in you, of a father in God to all who have been committed to your pastoral superintendence.

" On behalf of the Committee,

(Signed)   " ASHLEY."

Annexed is his Grace's reply :—

"Lambeth, April 11.

" My dear Lord Ashley,—Allow me to address to your
Lordship, as President of the Pastoral-Aid Society, the
sincere expression of my thanks to yourself and to the
Committee for the renewed testimony of regard which
they have sent to me on the occasion of my appointment
to the Primacy.

" I may say with truth that the highest gratification
which I have derived from that appointment, honourable
and important as it is, arises from the testimonies of the
same kind received from many quarters and from many
excellent persons, because I feel a confidence that they
who express themselves so favourably towards me will
assist me by their prayers in the faithful discharge of the
duties which lie before me.

" Among those duties none will appear to me more

urgent or more satisfactory to my own views of usefulness than that of promoting, as far as I have opportunity, the interests of the Pastoral-Aid Society, to which, both publicly and personally, I owe a great amount of obligation.

" I will request you to communicate to the Committee of the Society my thankful sense of the kindness of their address, and

    " I remain, my dear Lord,
     " With the greatest esteem,
      " Your Lordship's faithful and obliged,

       (Signed)   " J. B. CANTUAR.

" The Lord Ashley, &c."

The Committee recorded the decease of the Earl of Harrowby, K.G., one of the Society's most attached and liberal supporters. They were privileged to add that the present Earl of Harrowby, K.G., and the Bishops of Hereford and Manchester had become Vice-Patrons.

The Rev. Charles Clayton, having been appointed Tutor of his College, relinquished the office of Secretary of the Society, and the Rev. J. Hutton Pollexfen, M.A., of Queen's College, Cambridge, was appointed to act as his successor. Mr. Pollexfen entered upon his duties on the 1st of January, 1848. Mr. Clayton continued to afford assistance to the Society as its Honorary Secretary.

The Committee became involved in difficulty at this time, owing to the grants having been occu-

pied to an unprecedented extent, the proportion of
the vacancies being but one-fifteenth instead of,
as before, one-fourth. For example, in May, 1845,
there were 77 grants vacant out of 320, whereas
there were in this year only 24 out of 360. The
outlay, therefore, had increased in a corresponding
degree—that is to say, to the amount of about
5,000*l*. An urgent appeal was made for increased
funds.

MISSION TO MARINERS AND BOATMEN.

The work amongst mariners and boatmen in the
port of Gloucester was specially referred to in the
" Occasional Paper " (No. XXIII.) for April, 1848.
A similar Mission had been successfully carried
on for some years past in Worcester, under the
superintendence of the Rev. John Davies, by a
grant made for a chaplain by the Society. The
Rev. John Davies, with others, having matured
plans for the erection of a chapel at Gloucester,
forwarded an application to the Society for a grant
of 75*l*. per annum towards the chaplain's stipend.

A grant of that amount was accordingly made
to him. Mr. Davies voluntarily relinquished a
portion of the grant for the maintenance of a
minister in the Watermen's Church at Worcester,
and undertook to make up the deficiency from
other sources.

FOURTEENTH ANNIVERSARY.

The Fourteenth Annual Meeting was held in the large room, Exeter Hall, on Tuesday, the 8th of May, 1849, Lord Ashley in the chair. The speakers were the Revs. J. W. Brooks, John Davies, J. Hart, J. C. Miller, Chancellor Raikes, Hon. S. Waldegrave; Messrs. J. Colquhoun and F. Sandoz. The sermon was preached in St. Dunstan's Church, Fleet Street, London, by the Rev. W. Weldon Champneys, M.A., Rector of Whitechapel, London, upon the text 1 Cor. i. 24.

The Report stated that the Bishop of Sodor and Man and the Marquis of Blandford had accepted the office of Vice-Patrons.

APPOINTMENT OF ADDITIONAL ASSOCIATION SECRETARY.

The Committee recorded the appointment of an additional Association Secretary. The services of the Rev. Edward Walker, M.A., of Lincoln College, Oxford, and late Curate in charge of Silverdale, Lancashire, were engaged as Association Secretary for a new district, to be called the South Midland.

LARGE INCREASE OF SUBSCRIBERS.

Upwards of 200 clergymen, who never before supported the Society, became contributors to its funds during this year, and nearly 400 of the laity became subscribers to the Parent Society within the same period, independently of a much larger number who joined the Provincial Associations.

FIFTEENTH ANNIVERSARY.

The Fifteenth Annual Meeting of the Society was held in the large room, Exeter Hall, on Tuesday, the 7th of May, 1850, Lord Ashley in the chair.   The speakers were the Revs. James Bardsley, Robert Bickersteth, W. W. Champneys, John Richardson, J. C. Ryle, W. Sinclair, and E. Tottenham; and Mr. John Labouchere, Treasurer of the Society.

The sermon was preached in St. Dunstan's Church, Fleet Street, London, on Monday, the 6th of May, 1850, by the Rev. James Vaughan, M.A., Incumbent of Christ Church, Brighton, upon the text Eph. iv. 16.

NOMINATIONS.

The Committee took occasion to remark that the principle of the Society in requiring from incumbents full satisfaction as to the qualifications of those nominated had been prominently presented to the attention of its supporters for many years past, and had frequently called forth pointed expressions of approbation.

The examination of the testimonials of persons
intended to occupy the grants of the Society was
entrusted to the Clerical Sub-Committee, consisting
of twelve members (elected annually from the body
of clerical subscribers), who reported to the General
Committee the names of those only whose testimonials were considered satisfactory.   It was
stated that out of the comparatively few cases in
which nominations had not been sanctioned, the
Committee had, in the majority of instances,
received ultimately the cordial thanks of the
incumbents.

The Bishop's jurisdiction was said to be interfered with because the Society undertook to make
inquiry into the character of the persons on
whose account applications were made for its aid.
With reference to this subject the Committee
adverted to the speech of the late Bishop of
Lichfield delivered at the Annual Meeting of the
Society in 1841 :—" This inquiry. . . . is
invariably made before the person is nominated
to the Bishop. When an incumbent desires to
procure aid from this Society, the Committee
desire to be made acquainted with the name of the
individual in whose behalf aid is sought, and
inquiries are made by a clerical sub-committee of
this Society into the character and qualifications
of the party so named ; and what are these
inquiries ? The Committee do not inquire, as

has been truly said, whether the party is a Cal-
vinist or an anti-Calvinist, but whether, from his
previous life, habits, and conversation, he is likely
to be a faithful minister of the Gospel—whether,
if he enters into the sacred ministry, he is likely
to preach the Gospel of Christ faithfully and without reserve ; and when these inquiries are made,
when the Committee are satisfied of the qualifications of the curate, he is then nominated by the
incumbent to the Bishop, and not till then ; and
it rests with the Bishop to accept or refuse the
testimonials he produces.   Therefore I repeat that
the jurisdiction of the Bishop is in no degree
denied or interfered with. . . . In considering
this subject, it ought not to be forgotten that the
Pastoral-Aid Society has only a very limited
income, and that it can only meet a very small
proportion of the numerous applications for its
assistance ; the Committee, therefore, are not only
justified but it is their duty to have regard to the
qualifications of those to whom they give its aid,
and for that purpose the inquiry which I have
alluded to is absolutely necessary, and we owe to it
the very first principle of the Society, which is, to
proclaim the Gospel of Christ as widely and as
efficiently as possible."

The Committee recorded the decease during this
year of two of the Vice-Patrons of the Society, the
Bishops of Llandaff and Norwich. They also

expressed their regret that the Bishop of Manchester had withdrawn from the Society.

They had much pleasure in announcing that the Bishops of Chester, Llandaff, Victoria, and Rupert's Land had become Vice-Patrons of the Society.

With regard to Association proceedings, the Report stated that the Rev. Edward Walker, M.A., Association Secretary for the South Midland District, having been presented to a living in Manchester, the Committee had to record with regret the loss of his valuable services. A temporary engagement was entered into with the Rev. William Bruce, Incumbent of the Wicker Parish, Sheffield.

MRS. FRANK'S LEGACY.

The receipts for this year included a legacy of 5,000*l*. Three per Cent. Consols, bequeathed by the late Mrs. Elizabeth Frank, who during her life had been a most liberal contributor to the Society's funds. The stock, which was transferred to the Treasurer a few days before the close of the financial year, on being sold, realized the sum of 4,800*l*.

The Committee did not consider themselves justified in treating Mrs. E. Frank's legacy as a part of the regular income, and they therefore invested it in Long Annuities, terminating in

1860, which would yield until that date 590*l.* per annum. In taking this step the Committee followed the course which had already received the sanction and approval of the Society in respect of the principal portion of the legacy of the late Mr. John Scott.

PUBLICATIONS FOR THE YOUNG.

In the Occasional Paper No. XXVII., for September, 1849, special attention was called to the importance of enlisting the sympathies of the young in the Society's operations. Papers on this subject had been prepared—viz., " Suggestions on the subject of Juvenile Associations ; " and two "Addresses to the Young respecting the Church Pastoral-Aid Society "—one written by the Rev. W. Weldon Champneys, Rector of Whitechapel ; the other by a member of the Committee.

SIXTEENTH ANNIVERSARY.

The Sixteenth Annual Meeting of the Society was held in the large room, Exeter Hall, on Tuesday, 13th of May, 1851, the Earl of Shaftesbury, K.G., in the chair. The speakers were the Earls of Harrowby and Waldegrave ; the Revs. W. Crump, E. Hoare, J. C. Miller, T. Nolan, Hugh Stowell, and J. H. Titcomb; and Mr. J. Rand. The sermon was preached in St. Dunstan's Church, Fleet Street, London, on Monday, 12th May, 1851, by the Rev. Robert Bickersteth, M.A., Incumbent of St. John's, Clapham, upon the words of the Gospel, St. Matthew v. 13.

The Committee recorded the decease of Lord Bexley, one of the Vice-Patrons of the Society. The Report also stated that the Rev. William Bruce had resigned the Association Secretaryship of the South Midland District.

The Rev. Edward J. Speck, Curate of Stoke Goldington, Buckinghamshire, was appointed Secretary of the Society, in the room of the Rev. J. H. Pollexfen, who had been obliged, through ill-health, to resign that office.

The Committee referred in the Quarterly Paper No. XXX., for October, 1850, to a valuable letter addressed to the Bishop of Llandaff by Archdeacon Thomas Williams, "On the peculiar condition and wants of the Diocese." The attention of the Committee had for some time past been directed to the state of some of the mining districts of South Wales. The difficulty of providing for the spiritual instruction of the Welsh people arose from the fact that, though forming one community, they spoke different languages.

SEVENTEENTH ANNIVERSARY.

The Seventeenth Annual Meeting was held in the large room, Exeter Hall, London, on Tuesday, May 11th, 1852, the Earl of Shaftesbury, K.G., in the chair. The speakers were the Revs. W. Bruce,

G

W. Cadman, E. Hoare, C. Kemble, W. Pollock, J. C. Ryle, and Daniel Wilson; and Sir John Kennaway, Bart., and P. F. O'Malley, Esq., Q.C. The sermon was preached in St. Dunstan's Church, Fleet Street, London, on the 10th of May, 1852, by the Rev. Edward Hoare, Incumbent of Christ Church, Ramsgate, upon the text Ephesians iv. 11—13.

EIGHTEENTH ANNIVERSARY.

The Eighteenth Annual Meeting was held in the large room, Exeter Hall, on Tuesday, 10th of May, 1853, the Earl of Shaftesbury, K.G., in the chair. The speakers were the Bishops of Llandaff and Winchester, the Earl Waldegrave and Lord Haddo; the Revs. T. C. Cowan, Francis Close, J. Richardson, H. Stowell, and W. Wilkinson. The sermon was preached in St. Dunstan's Church, Fleet Street, London, on the 9th of May, 1853, by the Rev. W. Cadman, Incumbent of St. George's, Southwark, London.

Under the head of " Patronage," the Report stated that the Committee had great pleasure in adding to the list of Vice-Patrons the name of the Right Rev. Dr. Jackson, lately translated to the See of Lincoln.

BISHOP OF OXFORD (WILBERFORCE) WITHDRAWS FROM SOCIETY.

The Committee were requested by the Bishop of Oxford to remove his name from the list of members and officers of the Society.

MRS. BECKER'S LEGACY.

A legacy of 3,000*l.* of the late Mrs. Becker, of Bath, bequeathed " for the benefit of the Bath district," was this year notified.

NEEDS OF WALES.

The subject of the spiritual necessities of Wales was again prominently brought forward in the Report. The Committee stated that the people of the Principality were greatly indebted to the zeal and energy of the Bishop of Llandaff for the formation of the Llandaff Diocesan Society, which had effected so much for the benefit of the Church in that diocese. It was instituted not as antagonistic to, or in any way to sup-plant the societies already labouring in Wales, but rather to co-operate with them in a field so greatly needing labourers. The Bishop of Llandaff had referred in laudatory terms to the great debt which his diocese owed to the Church Pastoral-Aid Society.

APPOINTMENT OF WELSH-SPEAKING SECRETARY.

The Committee had long felt that it would be desirable to have a Welsh-speaking Clerical Association Secretary in the Principality (to which grants were made to the amount of 2,810*l.* an-nually), both for the advocacy of the Society's claims, as well as for correspondence with them-

G 2

selves. They accordingly appointed the Rev.
Thomas Walters, Curate of Kilvey, to that office.

SABBATH OBSERVANCE—MEMORIAL TO EARL OF DERBY.

The Committee, in the Occasional Paper No.
XXXVII., for January, 1853, expressed their conviction that much of the iniquity abounding in the
country was to be attributed to the desecration
of the Sabbath. . . . The Committee believed
that the cause of Sabbath observance was one
which concerned us, not as individuals merely,
but as a nation. It was, therefore, with deep
regret that they viewed a scheme which must
inevitably tend to diminish the sanctity of the
Lord's-day, and open the door to its national profanation. The great aim of the Church Pastoral-
Aid Society had ever been to confer inestimable
blessings upon the country by extending the privilege of the Christian Sabbath ; it already provided 570 additional public services every Lord's-
day.

It was felt that some strong measures should
be made to hinder, if possible, the completion of
a design fraught with such evil consequences.

It was, therefore, resolved to present the
following Memorial to the Prime Minister :—

" *To the Right Honourable the Earl of Derby, the
First Lord of Her Majesty's Treasury,*

" *The Memorial of the President and Committee of the Church Pastoral-Aid Society*

"*Sheweth*

"*That your memorialists distinctly recognise the Divine appointment and the universal and perpetual obligation of the Sabbath as 'made for man,' to be a day of rest, of sanctity, and of blessing. They believe that the sacred observance of the Lord's-day brings national as well as individual blessings. To this recognition of the Divine law they trace the elevated position which England has so long held amongst the nations of the earth.*

"*While they could not but admire the original conception, and the satisfactory execution of the Crystal Palace, in Hyde Park, your Petitioners regarded it with far deeper interest, as affording to our Continental neighbours the noble example of a nation fearing God, by making His law paramount to every other consideration, in the closing of the Exhibition throughout the entire of that day which He hath commanded to be kept holy.*

"*Your Memorialists are deeply and painfully anxious lest the new Crystal Palace about to be erected at Sydenham, in an enlarged and more enduring form, may, in striking contrast to the former, become the means of an extensive and fearful desecration of the Sabbath, should the building and gardens be allowed to be open on any part of that sacred day.*

" *Believing it to be the duty of a Christian Go-*
vernment to secure to all its subjects rest from labour,
and opportunity to worship God on His own day,
they tremble at the contemplation of the thousands
who will be deprived of this privilege and blessing
if called on to furnish to the multitudes who will
throng to the scene of amusement; and at the prece-
dent which will thereby be established for the
familiarizing the public mind with national acts of
Sabbath profanation.

" *Your Memorialists, as the Directors of a Society*
which has for many years been engaged in supplying
to the country large numbers of additional clergy-
men, whose labours have been greatly honoured of
God, in the promotion of religion and morality, and
especially the better observance of the Sabbath,
humbly, but most solemnly and earnestly, entreat
Her Majesty's Government not to grant a Charter
of Incorporation to the Crystal Palace Company
without specifically requiring that both the Palace
and Gardens be closed to the public on the Lord's-
day.

(Signed)   " SHAFTESBURY."

NINETEENTH ANNIVERSARY.

The Nineteenth Annual Meeting of the Society
was held in the large room, Exeter Hall, on May
9th, 1854, the Earl of Shaftesbury, K.G., in the
chair. The speakers were Bishop Carr, the Revs.

W. Bruce, George Lea, J. C. Miller, S. Minton, Hugh Stowell, and the Hon. M. Villiers and Mr. Robert Baxter. The sermon was preached by the Rev. C. J. P. Eyre, M.A., Incumbent of St. Mary's, Bury St. Edmund's, upon the text 2 Chron. xvii. 9, 10.

" HOME RECORD FOR THE YOUNG."

The Occasional Papers at this time contained an advertisement calling the attention of the friends of the Society to " *The Home Record for the Young*," a quarterly publication, edited by the Rev. W. Bruce, St. James's, Bristol. Sold by Messrs. Seeley, London ; Mr. Jones, Bristol ; and at the offices of the Society.

CHURCH BUILDING.

The Occasional Paper No. XLI., for April, 1854, referred in the following terms to the results of the Society's aid in respect of church building :— " The Committee cannot but express their belief that the operations of the Church Pastoral-Aid Society had materially promoted and encouraged the great work of church extension which had of late years been effected, and they direct attention to the fact that the grants of the Society have led to the erection, opening, or keeping open of 152 churches and chapels ; and in districts at present receiving the Society's aid there are now

184 rooms licensed for the celebration of Divine
service. It is known that many of these rooms
are the centres of contemplated parishes, and it is
more than probable that in every instance a church
will in due time take the place of the present
accommodation."

TWENTIETH ANNIVERSARY.

The Twentieth Annual Meeting of the Society
was held in the large room, Exeter Hall, on Tuesday, 5th of May, 1855, the Earl of Shaftesbury,
K.G., in the chair. The speakers were the Bishops
of Winchester and Melbourne, the Revs. D. T.
Barry, Canon Champneys, J. B. Jebb, W. C.
Magee, Canon Miller, and W. Wilkinson, and the
Marquis of Blandford. The sermon was preached
by the Rev. J. C. Miller, M.A., Honorary Canon
of Winchester, Rector of St. Martin's, Birmingham,
and Chaplain to Lord Calthorpe, upon the words
of the Gospel, St. Mark xii. 37.

The Report announced that the Bishops of
Sydney and Mauritius had accepted the office of
Vice-Patrons.

TWENTY-FIRST ANNIVERSARY.

The Twenty-first Annual Meeting was held in the
Freemasons' Hall, London, on Wednesday, May 8th,
1856, the Earl of Shaftesbury, K.G., in the chair.
The speakers were the Revs. W. R. B. Arthy,

C. Clayton, J. B. Marsden, J. C. Ryle, Hugh
Stowell, and W. Wilkinson. The sermon was
preached in St. Dunstan's Church, Fleet Street,
London, on Wednesday, the 7th of May, 1856, by
the Rev. William Bruce, M.A., Incumbent of St.
James's, Bristol, upon the words of the Gospel,
St. John iv. 34, 35.

CHURCH ACCOMMODATION.

The Report contained numerous statistics as to
the increase of the population of England and
Wales, and the means taken to provide the means
of grace. It appeared that since the year 1801 the
addition to the population of England and Wales
alone had been at least 6,500,000, and the whole
increase of church accommodation provided by the
State within that period, according to the 18th
Report of the Church Building Commissioners,
amounted to 225 churches, affording accommodation for 297,912, or less than one-twentieth of the
increased population. When the *metropolitan*
necessities were ascertained, the Bishop of London
immediately took measures for supplying them by
proposing to build at once *fifty* new churches by a
general subscription. The Bishop said in the
course of his circular, " Within the last fifty years
the population had increased from 9,000,000 to
nearly 18,000,000, while provision had been made
for additional church accommodation for not more

than one-tenth of the additional population, at least in great towns throughout the country."

TWENTY-SECOND ANNIVERSARY.

The Twenty-second Annual Meeting was held in the large room, Exeter Hall, on Tuesday, May 12th, 1857, the Earl of Shaftesbury, K.G., in the chair. The speakers were the Bishop of Carlisle, the Revs. H. Barne, T. R. Birks, W. Cadman, E. Hoare, R. E. Roberts, and Dr. Tyng.

The sermon was preached in St. Dunstan's Church, Fleet Street, London, on the 11th of May, 1857, by the Bishop of Carlisle, upon the words of the Gospel of St. Matthew ix. 35.

The Report announced that the Prelates who had been elevated during the past year to the Episcopal Bench, the Bishops of London, Gloucester and Bristol, Ripon, and Graham's Town, had accepted the office of Vice-Patrons.

LARGE INCOME.

With feelings of great thankfulness, the Committee recorded the largest annual income which the Society had yet received, the total receipts being 41,708l. 5s. 9d., a sum exceeding that of the year 1856 by 4,443l. 7s., and of any previous year by 1,479l. 18s, 9d. Of this augmentation, no less than 1,933l. 3s. 7d. had been derived from donations, subscriptions, and associations, which the Committee regarded as very satisfactory, since these were the sources of income on which they mainly relied for annually increasing supplies to extend the operations of the Society.

TWENTY-THIRD ANNIVERSARY.

The Twenty-third Annual Meeting was held in the large room, Exeter Hall, London, on Tuesday, May 11th, 1858, the Earl of Shaftesbury, K.G., in the chair. The speakers were the Bishop of Ripon, the Revs. R. Allen, James Bardsley, E. Garbett, T. M. Macdonald, Dr. Miller, and Hugh Stowell. The sermon was preached in St. Dunstan's Church, Fleet Street, London, by the Rev. J. B. Marsden, M.A., Incumbent of St. Peter's, Birmingham, upon the text 2 Kings ii. 21.

STATISTICS OF POPULATION SINCE 1066.

The Annual Report stated that the principal cause of the existing spiritual destitution had been the enormous increase of the population, especially since the beginning of the present century, as contrasted with the almost stationary condition of the people at earlier periods of our history. The number of the population at remote periods could not be determined with entire accuracy; still there were accredited estimates which assigned to England and Wales the numbers contained in the following table :—

1066	.	(nearly)	.	2,000,000
1377	.	.	. .	2,500,000

1570	.	(over)	.	4,000,000
1700	.	.	.	6,000,000
1750	.	.	.	6,500,000
1801	.	(census returns)	8,872,710
1841	.	.	.	15,906,741
1851	.	.	.	17,905,831

It would thus be seen that the population had doubled itself in the first half of the nineteenth century; and its annual increase, after the necessary deductions for emigration were made, had exceeded 200,000. Since the census of 1851, the addition to the population of the metropolis has been 254,600, and its annual progress is now 60,000.

While the population had been advancing with such rapid strides, the resources of the clergy had remained nearly stationary; and even with the best arrangements that could be made, the finances of the Church of England were inadequate to the performance of the duty which devolved upon it as the instructor of the people.

INSUFFICIENCY OF CLERICAL INCOMES.

It appeared from the Report of the Ecclesiastical Commissioners for 1835 that there were 297 benefices in England and Wales under 50l. per annum; 1,629 benefices more than 50l. yet under 100l.; 1,602, above 100l. but under 150l.; and 1,354, above 150l. but under 200l. per annum;

there were therefore nearly 5,000 with incomes
varying from less than 200*l.* to even less than 50*l.*
a year; and since that period many new districts
had been formed with endowments lamentably
insufficient.

The Committee observed that the difficulties of
many of the clergy were often greatly increased by
the necessity of contributing to the expenses inci-
dent to the maintenance of public worship. In cities
and wealthy town parishes, voluntary funds might
be raised for this purpose; but in poor or country
parishes it was difficult to do this, and altogether
impossible to provide additional pastors for the
thousands who were destitute of the means of
grace. In such cases the value of the Society
was clearly seen.

The Report stated that the Committee had
much pleasure in announcing that the Bishops of
Calcutta and Sierra Leone had accepted the office
of Vice-Patrons. The decease of the late Bishop
of Calcutta was recorded.

Under the head of "Funds" the Committee
observed that "it was satisfactory and encouraging to know that, notwithstanding the commercial
difficulties of the past year, and the large demands
of the 'Indian Relief Fund' upon the charity of
the nation, the contributions from some Auxiliaries
had been larger in amount than those of any former
years. The Committee were happy in having this

opportunity of testifying to the unwearied exertions of many friends to increase the funds of the Society; if the like zeal and untiring effort were more generally called into exercise, there would be little difficulty in raising the Society's income to the 50,000l. which, at the last anniversary, was so earnestly pleaded for." It was added, "The Committee cannot refrain from again urging on all clergymen receiving grants, the obligation under which they lie, to exert themselves to the very utmost to aid the funds of this Protestant and Evangelical Society. It will be a source of deep regret to them to reduce the amount of any such existing grants; yet such a course will, in several cases, be imperatively necessary, unless the returns from those districts bear a more just proportion to the great benefits bestowed."

The total amount for which the Society was at this time pledged was 45,815l. per annum.

TWENTY-FOURTH ANNIVERSARY.

The Twenty-fourth Annual Meeting of the Society was held in St. James's Hall, Piccadilly, London, on Thursday, May 5th, 1859, the Earl of Shaftesbury, K.G., in the chair. The speakers were the Bishop of Carlisle, the Revs. E. Auriol, W. C. Magee, W. McCall, Canon Miller, and T. Nolan.

The sermon was preached in St. Dunstan's

Church, Fleet Street, London, on the 4th of May,
1859, by the Rev. James Bardsley, M.A., Rector
of Ann's, Manchester, upon the text St. James
i. 18.

BIRMINGHAM.

The spiritual destitution of *Birmingham* formed
the leading subject of the "Occasional Paper"
No. LIV., for October, 1858. It was stated that,
"during the last seven years, eight new churches
had been consecrated in the Borough of Birmingham or its immediate suburbs, in addition to the
opening of the cemetery church, as a place of
worship, the restoration of St. Martin's spire, and
the enlargement of the two older churches in
Edgbaston." It was in connection with such a
movement that the value of the Church Pastoral-
Aid Society was strikingly seen. . . . . Of
the eight new churches above-named, five were,
at this time, receiving grants. There were thirty-
five grants made to seventeen incumbents; fifteen
for curates and twenty for lay agents, at a cost
to the Society of 2,745*l.* The population of the
districts thus aided was 205,150. The returns
from the Birmingham Association were but small,
amounting for the year ending March, 1858, to
only 861*l.*

The results which had attended the operations
of the Society in Birmingham had been of an en-

couraging character. Fifteen curates and twenty lay assistants were supported in that town; and by their means fifty-six additional Church and School Services and Weekly Cottage Lectures were provided.

BRADFORD.

Special mention was made in the Occasional Paper No. LV., for January, 1859, of the town of Bradford. Few places, it was remarked, had received a greater share of the Society's assistance; and possibly none had required it more. In 1839 . . . . several grants were made for curates to take charge of districts. Their work was quite of a missionary character; in some instances even suitable rooms for Divine worship could scarcely be obtained. These early grants had led to the erection of churches, and the assignment of ecclesiastical districts. In the Borough of Bradford there were at this time, besides the parish church, nine district churches, affording altogether accommodation for about 9,000. Exclusive of the population attached to these district churches, between 70,000 and 80,000 still devolved on the Mother Church. Fifteen grants were in this year made to Bradford—twelve for curates and three for lay assistants. The expense to the Society was 1,290*l.*, while the returns from the auxiliary did not exceed 300*l.*

The Twenty-fifth Annual Meeting of the Society was held in St. James's Hall, Piccadilly, London, on Thursday, the 3rd of May, 1860, the Earl of Shaftesbury, K.G., in the chair. The speakers were the Bishops of Ripon and Sierra Leone; the Revs. E. Hoare, J. B. Marsden, Dr. Robinson, and Hugh Stowell. The sermon was preached on the 2nd of May, 1860, in St. Dunstan's Church, Fleet-street, London, by the Bishop of Bangor, upon the text Ephesians iii. 12.

The Report referred to the decease of Earl Earl Waldegrave, a Vice-Patron of the Society; and announced that the Bishops of Bangor, Rochester, and Sierra Leone had accepted the office of Vice-Patrons.

PROPOSAL TO APPOINT ORGANIZING SECRETARIES.

The Committee this year had under their consideration the important question as to the best means of increasing the efficiency of the work in the several Association districts, so as to secure larger returns to the Society's funds. There were two difficulties which materially impeded the usefulness of the Association Secretaries. The first, that of not obtaining to the extent that might be expected, the support of the body of the Evangelical clergy; and the second, in not being able to arrange for the advocacy of the Society in neigh-

H

bouring parishes at the same time. The consequence was, that increased expenditure was incurred by deputations having to visit the same localities at different periods of the year. The Committee had long felt that the size of the districts constituted another difficulty which greatly prevented the secretaries from breaking up fresh ground. It was therefore resolved to adopt the experiment of appointing a few *Organizing Secretaries* in different parts of the country. Incumbents of parishes had been found suitable in every way for such a post, and willing for 50*l.* a year and their travelling expenses to undertake within a given circuit the deputation arrangements—such as providing for sermons and meetings. and rendering some assistance themselves, circulating the reports and papers, and specially endeavouring to gain additional support for the Society. The design was to contract the districts for the Association Secretaries, and to increase the funds by entering on fresh ground. *The arrangement was intended to be an experimental one, and the continuance of such an agency would depend upon the results.*

Four gentlemen were appointed to this office —three to labour in the northern district, and to have charge of districts in the neighbourhoods of Liverpool, Manchester, and Leeds; and the fourth to undertake work in the counties of Norfolk and Suffolk.

STATEMENT OF INCOME AND NUMBER OF GRANTS.

Special attention was drawn to the following table, presenting a comparative view of the income and number of grants for curates and lay agents for the last few years :—

—	Income	Number of Grants		Total
		Curates	Lay assistants	
	£ s. d.			
1852-53	40,228 7 0	317	115	432
1853-54	38,574 17 9	343	143	486
1854-55	38,173 7 0	341	145	486
1855-56	37,264 18 9	343	146	489
1856-57	41,708 5 9	374	163	537
1857-58	41,109 9 8	376	163	539
1858-59	43,856 15 8	391	154	545
1859-60	41,475 18 9	401	156	557

AID TO WALES.

The Occasional Paper No. LVIII., for January, 1860, consisted of an earnest appeal for funds to supply the Principality with additional labourers. The Society's grants at this time in Wales—chiefly South Wales—were for forty curates and seven lay assistants at a cost of 3,560l. The returns from associations in the Principality amounted, for 1859-60, to 1,178l.

H 2

NOTTINGHAM.

The Occasional Paper No. LIX., for April, 1860, contained accounts of the spiritual destitution of Nottingham, and stated that the Society's grants to that town and its neighbourhood were for eight curates and one lay agent, and amounted to 760*l.* per annum. The returns from the Association during the past year had been only 274*l.*

TWENTY-SIXTH ANNIVERSARY.

The Twenty-sixth Annual Meeting of the Society was held in St. James's Hall, Piccadilly, on Thursday, May 2nd, 1861, the Earl of Shaftesbury, K.G., in the chair. The speakers were the Bishop of London, the Revs. James Bardsley, O. Clayton, G. T. Fox, D. Howell, and J. C. Ryle, and Mr. J. C. Colquhoun. The sermon was preached in St. Dunstan's Church, Fleet Street, London, on the 1st of May, 1861, by the Rev. T. R. Birks, M.A., Rector of Kelshall, Herts, and Examining Chaplain to the Bishop of Durham, upon the text, Romans xvi. 25-27.

The Society this year completed the twenty-fifth year of its existence, and the Committee felt that the event called for their special gratitude and thanksgiving to Almighty God.

COMPARATIVE SMALLNESS OF GRANTS OF PUBLIC MONEY TOWARDS RELIEF OF SPIRITUAL DESTITUTION.

The Report observed that "direct grants of

public money towards the relief of the spiritual destitution of the country could not, under existing circumstances, be expected." The Ecclesiastical Commissioners were charged with a redistribution of Church revenues, but the process was necessarily slow. Private liberality, when stimulated by piety, showed itself to be more efficient than public grants. The progress of church building was a proof in point. For the first thirty years of the present century private benefactions and public grants were nearly equal, the former yielding about 1,800,000*l.* and the latter 1,200,000*l.*; the product was 500 churches. In the twenty years ensuing the grants from public money barely exceeded half a million, whereas private subscriptions mounted up to more than five millions and a-half; and 2,029 churches arose in consequence. . . . The providing ministerial agency and raising the spiritual instead of the material church, in the first instance, was the best mode of advancing church building. Anything which tended to work out the parochial system by allotting a manageable district to one clergyman was to be regarded as a great boon. . . . A considerable number of the new churches which had of late years sprung up possessed very small endowments, and in many instances none whatever. The ministers of such churches were altogether dependent upon pew rents. *This system might suffice for wealthy districts,*

*but it did not meet the wants of the poor, who were
unable to pay for seats.* . . . The income
which the clergy derived from these new churches
was often deplorably insufficient. The Committee
had never felt that because these slender endowments must necessarily be supplemented by pew-
rents, therefore the Society's assistance should not
be afforded, for, generally speaking, such churches
were in districts which imperatively called for
help.

"ESSAYS AND REVIEWS"—SPEECH OF BISHOP OF RIPON.

The Report referred, in terms of approval, to a
speech of the Bishop of Ripon, delivered at the
Annual Meeting of the Bradford Auxiliary, with
reference to the publication of *"Essays and
Reviews."*

The Bishop observed:—"It was a cause of
thankfulness to God that, without one dissenting
voice, the Bishops of the Church of England to a
man had pronounced an emphatic condemnation
of the infamous opinions propounded in these
'Essays and Reviews.' . . . He did consider
it the most cruel wound that could have been
inflicted in the side of the Church of England,
that the authors of these *'Essays and Reviews'*
should have written and published what infidel
lecturers were but too glad to substitute for their

own arguments in support of their sceptical opinions. It was indeed a cruel wound to the Church of England that such a publication should emanate, not from those who were her open and avowed enemies, but from those whose professed principles and position were in such diametrical opposition. *For these reasons, amongst others, he considered that the principle to which he had adverted of the Church Pastoral-Aid Society was one of extreme value, in perfect harmony with the discipline of our Church, and one which was especially needed at the present day.*"

Under the head of "*Patronage*," the Committee stated that the Bishop of Carlisle had accepted the office of Vice-Patron of the Society.

WORKING EXPENSES OF RELIGIOUS SOCIETIES.

The Report for this year contained an appendix on the subject of "*the working expenses of religious Societies*." The Committee observed "that a more than usual degree of attention had, during the last two or three years, been directed to this subject. The amount was large, but the real question was whether it was necessarily so. Expressions of dissatisfaction came, with scarcely an exception, from persons who had had no experience in managing such Societies, and their opinions were consequently theoretical.

In the early part of this year a subscriber to the

Society withdrew his subscription on the ground of expensive management, and transferred it to a kindred Society, at the same time expressing his opinion that the employment of Association Secretaries, at fixed salaries, was a mistake, and cost 1,800*l.* a year. He complained, further, that the printing expenses were not reduced by following the example of another great Society, which did not print sermons, and issued subscription-lists only on fly-sheets for different localities.

These remarks having come under the notice of a member of the Society, he examined the balance-sheets of four Societies referred to on that occasion, and laid the results of his inquiries before the Committee, which appeared to them to be of sufficient interest and importance to be printed and circulated.

The objections were classed under two heads. First. In comparison with other Societies. Secondly. In principle, as to the fitness of the means adopted to secure the end in view.

First.—An examination of the balance-sheets of this and the four other Societies showed a percentage of office expenses and management, in proportion to the funds raised, as follows:— Pastoral-Aid Society, $11\frac{7}{10}$, and the four other Societies respectively, $11\frac{9}{10}$, $12\frac{3}{5}$, 13, and 17. In reference to the particular Society to which

the gentleman above alluded to transferred
his subscription, it appeared from their own
balance-sheet that the per-centage of expense
was greater than that of this Society, even
including in their receipts a sum of 798*l.*
received by a defaulting collector, which never
reached the treasury of the Society. It appeared
further, on examining the accounts of the Society,
whose example in the matter of printing was held
up for imitation, that that item amounted to
2,713*l.* against 640*l.* of this Society, or double the
amount *in proportion to income.* And it was also
found that the cost of printing the fly-sheets of
subscriptions amounted to 482*l., or more than the
whole cost of printing the report, sermon, and subscription-lists of the Pastoral-Aid Society put
together.*

The friends of the Society had, therefore, no
reason to be dissatisfied with the amount of office
expenses, *comparatively*, seeing that they were less
in proportion to income than those of any of the
Societies referred to by the complainant, and which
were supposed to be managed with the greatest
economy.

Secondly.—But perhaps the most important
point was the principle involved in maintaining
Association Secretaries at fixed salaries. *This
question*, the Committee affirmed, *was no longer
one of opinion or theory ; it had been already proved
by experience to be absolutely necessary.*

The Committee, in the early years of the Society, tried the plan of employing as Association Secretaries the incumbents of small parishes, to whom they supplied the means of keeping curates, in order that they might have leisure to work for the Society. *To say nothing of the inconsistency of a Pastoral-Aid Society systematically taking an incumbent from his parish, the plan was found, financially, to be a failure.* Such gentlemen could not do one most important part of the work for which Association Secretaries were engaged, and which they performed, namely, preaching from seventy to a hundred sermons annually on its behalf. But, further, the income of a kindred Society fell from 20,000*l.* to 15,000*l.*; at that time it had no Association Secretary. One was, however, appointed, and the result was so satisfactory, that in the following year the Committee resolved to appoint a second; they had since increased that sort of agency, and their income had reached 23,000*l.*

Again, another great Society, after existing above a century, had an income of only a few thousands, exclusive of Parliamentary Grant and Queen's Letters. On the withdrawal of those two sources of income, the Society was driven to the only measure which afforded the prospect of raising a large income from the country, namely, the appointment of travelling and paid organizing

secretaries. The result had been that they had
an income of 85,000*l.*, which, it was believed, was
double what it previously was, including Parliamentary Grant and Queen's Letters.   It was likewise to be noted that that Society, in addition to
Travelling Secretaries, employed twenty-five paid
Organizing Secretaries; and the *salaries of the
latter alone amounted to forty per cent. more than
the aggregate salaries of all the Association Secretaries of the Pastoral-Aid Society.*

BRISTOL.

The Occasional Paper No. LX., for October,
1860, sketched the history of the city of Bristol.
The Society at this time made twelve grants to
that city—ten for curates and two for lay agents.
The total cost of these grants to the Society was
990*l.*, and the amount received from the Bristol
auxiliary for the year ending 31st of March, 1860,
was 1,310*l.* 17*s.* 5*d.*

Bristol, therefore, returned more than the
amount which the Society expended on it, but the
relative claims of other parts of the country
obliged the Committee to consider the excess as
a free-will offering for other districts even more
destitute.

HULL, SHIELDS, AND NEWCASTLE-ON-TYNE.

The seaports of Hull, Shields, and Newcastle-
upon-Tyne formed the subject of the Occasional

Paper No. LXI., for January, 1861. The Committee earnestly appealed for increased funds to supply the means of grace to the populations of these towns.

Attention was drawn in the Occasional Paper No. LXII., for April, 1861, to the naval ports of Portsmouth and Chatham. In these towns the Society made grants for four curates and one lay agent at a cost of 411*l.* ; the Association returned in this year 84*l.* Since the Crimean War a great step had been taken in the spiritual improvement of our soldiers by the introduction of Scripture-readers into barracks and military hospitals. Three such labourers had been working most beneficially in the garrison at Chatham, and one, supported by the " Seamen's Mission Society," had lately been placed, under the superintendence of the curate, to labour amongst the sailors of the merchant service and the fishermen. To the Church Pastoral-Aid Society was given the privilege of bringing lay agency into practice as a systematic part of the machinery of the Church of England.

TWENTY-SEVENTH ANNIVERSARY.

The Twenty-seventh Annual Meeting of the Society was held in St. James's Hall, Piccadilly, London, on Thursday, 8th of May, 1862, the Earl

of Shaftesbury, K.G., in the chair. The speakers
were the Dean of Carlisle, the Revs. Charles
Kemble, G. Pettitt, Canon Savage, and Canon
Stowell. The sermon was preached by the Bishop
of Carlisle, in St. Dunstan's Church, Fleet Street,
London, on the 7th of May, 1862, upon the
words of the Gospel St. John, xii. 32, 33.

PRINCE CONSORT'S DEATH.

The Report referred to "the heartfelt sorrow
so plainly expressed on the occasion of the
decease of the lamented Prince Consort." It was
also remarked that, " not in the palace only was
the Lord's voice heard, but in the dwellings also
of ' the sons of toil ' ; and from our gracious
Queen, in the poignancy of her grief, to the
humblest of her subjects, the most lively sympathy was felt with the bereaved widows and
orphans of those who perished at Hartley Pit
and Gethin."

PATRONAGE.

The Committee had much pleasure in announc-
ing that the Bishops of Gloucester and Bristol,
Worcester, and Madras, had accepted the office of
Vice-Patrons of the Society.

FUNDS—MR. FOX'S OFFER.

Under the head of " Funds," the Committee
observed that the munificent donation of 1,000l.

which was offered by a valued friend at the anniversary in 1861, called forth a similar sum from another warm supporter of the Society and also other liberal contributions from those who had ever taken the liveliest interest in its operations. The total amount raised by means of the Special Fund was a little more than 3,000*l.* In making his offer, Mr. Fox fully expected that it would be more generally responded to, and that at least 10,000*l.* or 15,000*l.* would be raised to celebrate " the half jubilee year " of the Society.

The Committee, at this time, stood pledged to a sum of 50,000*l.* per annum. The total amount of funds raised during the past twenty-six years had been 761,975*l.*, of which sum, 69,749*l.* had been derived from legacies.

ASSOCIATION PROCEEDINGS.

The Committee reported that the experiment which was tried about two years previously of appointing *Organizing Secretaries* in different parts of the country had not generally succeeded. . . . It was evident that the formation of new associations required, not the partial, but the full time and strength of any person. The Rev. A. A. Nunn, of Parr, however, continued his office of Organizing Secretary, and was enabled to make such parochial arrangements as to allow of his rendering very efficient aid in carrying out the object in view.

It was observed that most valuable assistance might be afforded if several clergymen in every county could be prevailed upon to act as Honorary Secretaries, and to make, within a small circle around their respective parishes, the necessary arrangements for sermons and meetings. A few valued friends had consented thus to act, and the Committee augured encouraging results from their kind help.

It was announced that the Rev. A. P. Irwine, having been appointed to the Vicarage of Bingley, would shortly resign the office of Association Secretary for the Northern District.

AID TO PLYMOUTH, DEVONPORT, AND STONEHOUSE.

The Occasional Paper No. LXIII., for October, 1861, gave some results of the Society's aid in the towns of Plymouth, Devonport, and Stonehouse. The District of North Corner was singled out for special comment, and was said to be " to a large extent a very sink of iniquity." Grants were made in these towns for four curates and one lay assistant, benefiting a population of thirty-three thousand.

REV. J. DAVIES' WORK AT GLOUCESTER.

The Quarterly Paper No. LXIV., for January, 1862, contained numerous statistics of church accommodation in the city of Gloucester. The efforts of the Rev. John Davies, at Runcorn and other places, were again alluded to. Mr. Davies laboured with much success for the spiritual benefit of this class of men at Worcester. He received a grant from the Society for the maintenance of a minister in the *Waterman's Church* there.

In 1848 Mr. Davies' co-operation was invited by some Christian friends at Gloucester. He matured their plans for the erection of a chapel on a piece of ground near the docks, and voluntarily relinquishing a portion of his own grant, the incumbent in whose district the chapel was erected applied to the Society for 75*l.* a year to meet a similar sum raised locally for a chaplain's stipend. The care of the seamen and watermen, wherever they could be met with, on the quays, on board ship, in the Sailors' Homes and lodging-houses, constituted the parish of the chaplain.

SUMS RAISED BY CARDS AND BOXES.

It was stated in the Quarterly Paper No. LXV., for April, 1862, that the total amount raised by means of *collecting cards and boxes* during the year ending the 31st March last, amounted to 1,829*l.*

SIR ROBERT PEEL'S ACT.

This paper also contained the following statement with reference to Sir Robert Peel's Act:—" It has been sometimes supposed that this Act for the sub-division of large parishes has superseded the necessity for any extension of the Society's operations; such a view is altogether erroneous; the Act in question has been most important, but in numbers of the newly-formed districts the population ranges from 5,000 to 8,000; the continuance of the Society's aid is therefore needed now more than ever."

TWENTY-EIGHTH ANNIVERSARY.

The Twenty-eighth Annual Meeting of the Society was held in St. James's Hall, Piccadilly, London, on Thursday, May 7th, 1863, the Earl of Shaftesbury, K.G., in the chair. The speakers were the Bishop of Goulburn, the Revs. B. Addison, James Bardsley, Talbot Greaves, and H. Powell. The sermon was preached in St. Dunstan's Church, Fleet Street, London, by the Dean of Carlisle, upon the text Deut. xviii. 15.

MARRIAGE OF PRINCE OF WALES.

With reference to the marriage of the Prince of Wales, the Committee, after alluding to the close connection between the happiness of princes and the liberty of their subjects, went on to remark in their report, " most touchingly was this unanimous feeling of respect seen in the national mourning for the death of the Prince Consort, and it found its overwhelming expression in joy for the wedding

I

of the young Prince, his son. The Divine precept was obeyed, '*Weep with them that weep*,' and '*Rejoice with them that do rejoice.*' "

The CENSUS TABLES, it was stated, revealed the striking fact of the flow of population to the suburbs of great cities.......The wealthier classes, generally speaking, flocked to the suburbs, whilst those remaining in the centres of our great cities were of the poorer classes, a circumstance which tended to increase the difficulties of the clergy. London had nearly trebled its population during the present century, having advanced from 958,863 in 1801, to 2,803,989 in 1861.

It was an appalling consideration that nearly one million of the population of the metropolis attended no place of worship on the Lord's-day. Figures were given in the Census Papers of 1851 on this subject; and according to the evidence taken by a Select Committee of the House of Lords, in 1859, notwithstanding all that had been done to induce attendance since 1851, there were 68 per cent. absent in Southwark, and 60 per cent. in Lambeth, of the adult population capable of attending the means of grace.

It was, for the most part, amongst the vast masses in the manufacturing districts, and the densely-thronged parishes of large towns and cities, that the Society's grants were made, and, with very rare exceptions, the benefices thus aided were very inadequately endowed. In wealthy suburbs pew-rents afforded a sufficient maintenance for the minister, but amongst poor populations this source of income was both small and uncertain, hence the importance of securing a permanent provision for the ministrations of religion.

INCOME OF BENEFICES.

It was stated that in the first Report of the Ecclesiastical Commissioners, published in 1835, there were 3,528 benefices with incomes under 150*l.* a year. There had been great changes since that return was made. In the last Report of this body, dated 26th February, 1863, it was recorded that—

" The total number of benefices and districts augmented and endowed by the Commissioners amounts to 1,430; and the total permanent charge upon the ' Common Fund,' inclusive of grants in respect of benefactions paid to them, exceeds the sum of 107,700*l.* per annum, besides 18,000*l.* per annum payable to the Governors of Queen Anne's Bounty, to make immediate provision for additional cases."

These 1,430 included 293 Peel districts, of which 266 had been already provided with churches, and endowed with 150*l.* a-year. The remaining 1,164 which had been augmented or

endowed would no doubt include many of the
3,528 under 150l. a-year mentioned in the Ecclesiastical Commissioners' First Report, as well as
some new districts subsequently formed. And
many had been endowed by .private means. On
the other hand, if 80 churches per annum had
been built, say 2,200 since 1835, so many of them
were poorly endowed that the number under 150l.
a-year was probably as great at this time as it was
in 1835.

DECEASE OF ARCHBISHOP SUMNER AND MR. F. SANDOZ.

The Committee recorded the decease of Dr.
Sumner, Archbishop of Canterbury. As Bishop
of Chester, he was one of the earliest and most
strenuous of the Society's supporters ; and to his
patronage and wise counsel might be attributed,
under God, much of the success which attended
its early operations. When elevated to the
Primacy he still felt the liveliest interest in the
Society's proceedings, and was a liberal contributor
to its funds.

The Committee also recorded the decease of
Mr. Frederic Sandoz, to whose energy and zeal was
chiefly to be ascribed the institution of the
Society.

PATRONAGE.

It was announced that the Archbishops of Canterbury and York, and the Bishops of Gloucester

and Bristol and Goulburn, had accepted the office of Vice-Patrons of the Society.

ASSOCIATION PROCEEDINGS.

Under the head of "*Association Proceedings*," the Committee announced that the Rev. J. N. Grren-Armytage had been compelled, through declining health, to resign the office of Association Secretary for the South Midland District.

The Rev. W. Tatlock, Incumbent of Widnes, succeeded Mr. Armytage, and took up his residence at Gloucester.

The Rev. Richard Waters was appointed to the Northern District, which, for many years, was superintended by the Rev. A. P. Irwine, who still afforded his kind help as Honorary Secretary for the West Riding of Yorkshire.

The Committee were thankful to report that a few clergymen had undertaken to act as *Honorary Secretaries* in their respective neighbourhoods, and there was reason to believe that others would volunteer their services in this good work.

HARTLEY COLLIERY EXPLOSION.

The Quarterly Paper No. LXVI., for October, 1862, contained a wood engraving of the "Scene at Hartley Colliery after the Accident." To the several colliery districts in which these explosions occurred, the Society afforded assistance. An incumbent, in recording the great benefits of the grant for a curate which enabled him to institute *regular pastoral visitation* throughout his extended parish adjoining the Hartley district, thus wrote : —" In the late awful calamity at Hartley, I found the aid of a curate most invaluable, and I feel sure that many of the bereaved families would have lost the benefit of much spiritual consolation but for his kind assistance."

This Quarterly Paper treated especially of the spiritual destitution of the mining and manufacturing districts. It was stated that aid towards the support of 136 curates and 59 lay agents— *more than one-third of the whole agency supported by the Society*—was granted to Lancashire and the West Riding of Yorkshire.

COTTON FAMINE—AID TO LANCASHIRE AND CHESHIRE.

In the Quarterly Paper No. LXVII., for January, 1863, the subject of the Cotton Famine was discussed. Special attention was invited to the weekly returns of the Statistical Department of the Poor Law Board. Every week showed a large excess of pauperism over that which preceded it; the number of operatives in full work was constantly being reduced and the numbers of those on short time, or entirely thrown out of employment, was increasing ; the loss of wages was about 150,000*l.* a week, while the savings of the working classes were about exhausted. It was estimated that

before the winter months were over, there would
be at least 300,000 factory hands, representing
600,000 persons, dependent on allowances from
the Board of Guardians and Relief Committees.

In the very districts where distress at this time
so extensively prevailed, the Society commenced
its operations.........The following table showed
the amount of population in Lancashire and
Cheshire at this time benefited by the Society's
grants, the number of curates and lay agents, the
cost at which they were maintained, and the
amounts contributed last year from those counties
to the Society's funds :—

Counties	Population	Curates	Lay-agents	Cost to the Society	Amounts remitted to the Society
				£	£
Lancashire ...	702,689	73	40	8,700	4,180
Cheshire	180,721	23	12	2,695	847
	883,410	96	52	11,395	5,027

The subject of the Cotton Famine was continued in the Quarterly Paper No. LXVIII., for
April, 1863. It was observed that " the Society's
correspondents bore one and the same testimony
to the evident tokens that good was likely to

result from this terrible distress. Notwithstanding the loss of many of those comforts which their usual wages enabled the operatives to procure for themselves and their families, there was no murmuring, nor complaining, nor finding fault with others, but a calm and patient resignation, and a remarkable willingness to hear the Word of God."

TWENTY-NINTH ANNIVERSARY.

The Twenty-ninth Annual Meeting of the Society was held in St. James's Hall, Piccadilly, London, on Thursday, May 5th, 1864, the Earl of Shaftesbury, K.G., in the chair. The speakers were the Revs. Canon Boyd, W. Cadman, Canon Champneys, John Richardson, and Canon Stowell. The sermon was preached in St. Dunstan's Church, Fleet Street, London, on the 4th of May, 1864, by the Archbishop of York, upon the text Romans xiii. 11—14.

BISHOP OF LONDON'S FUND.

The Report referred to an important movement set on foot in 1863 by the Bishop of London for the relief of the religious wants of the diocese, when a resolution was adopted to raise for that purpose the sum of 1,000,000*l.* in the course of the ensuing ten years. A body of statistics had been collected respecting (1) The proportion of clergy to the population, and (2) The proportion of Church-room to population; and laid before a large and influential meeting of clergy, presided over by the Bishop. The Report read on that occasion stated that, adopting the standard of one clergyman to every 2,000 people, and of Church accommodation for one in four of the population, 500 additional clergy and 250,000 sittings would be needed, in order to bring the diocese up to the required standard of efficiency; and further that 6,000 male and female lay agents, and additional school accommodation for not less than 100,000 children, were also demanded. To accomplish all this, at least 3,000,000l. would be required, and the Bishop expressed a confident hope that, to effect so grand an object, even this sum would be raised.

The Committee, in the first year of its operations, made six grants—three for curates and three for lay agents—to the diocese of London. Since 1837 its agency had been annually increasing within the Metropolitan circle.

The Society had expended altogether in grants for curates and lay agents in London and the Metropolitan circle, the sum of 91,450l., thus apportioned :—

Diocese of London £63,460
Diocese of Winchester, within the
    Metropolitan circle 27,990
                              £91,450

AUGMENTATION OF BENEFICES.

The Committee took occasion to refer to the Report of the Ecclesiastical Commissioners (which had been recently published), detailing what had been already accomplished with regard to the augmentation of benefices, and stating that they were prepared to augment to 300*l.* a year the income of every benefice in public patronage, the population of which was, by the Census of 1861, not less than 8,000 souls. The Ecclesiastical Commissioners, it was remarked, expected within the next five years to raise to 300*l.* a year the income of every benefice under similar patronage with a population of 4,000. The Committee were thankful to know that several incumbents on their list had received during the past year an augmentation of income; and they rejoiced to find that many others would shortly be recipients of the same boon.

The Committee, in commenting upon what had been termed " the disgraceful poverty of the clerical profession," took occasion to observe that " the present rate of curates' salaries was still too low, and that they were fully alive to the evils arising out of a constant change of curates." Nevertheless, any measure for raising the stipends of curates generally was too important to be hastily adopted. . . . . The effect of any such measure on the finances and operations of the

Society was not to be overlooked. An additional
income of probably not less than 2,000l. per
annum would be required to carry out the
scheme.

TREASURERSHIP—DECEASE OF MR. J. LABOUCHERE—APPOINTMENT OF MR. H. S. THORNTON.

The Committee recorded the decease of Mr.
John Labouchere, Treasurer of the Society since
the date of its institution. Mr. Henry Sykes
Thornton was appointed his successor in that
office.

The Report further recorded the decease of
Admiral Sir Henry Hope, K.C.B., Mr. John
Pemberton Plumptre, Vice-Presidents of the
Society, the Rev. Francis Cunningham, and the
Rev. H. Hutton; also that the Bishops of Ely
and Peterborough had accepted the office of Vice-
Patrons.

ASSOCIATION PROCEEDINGS.

The Rev. George Despard, having been appointed Minister of St. Paul's, Kilburn, resigned
the office of Association Secretary for the South-
Eastern or London district. The Rev. C. H.
Miller was appointed his successor.

SOCIETY'S OPERATIONS FROM 1837 TO 1863.

The following table, exhibiting a comparative
view of the Society's operations from the year
after its institution to the 31st of March, 1863,

is taken from the Quarterly Paper No. LXIX., for October, 1863 :—

Dates	No. of parishes aided	No. of Grants for		Population benefited	Income of Society		
		Curates	Lay-agents		£	s.	d.
1837	68	58	13	542,865	7,363	11	0
1843	235	233	31	1,801,452	17,562	19	11
1853	369	341	132	2,675,129	40,228	7	0
1863	439	402	154	3,481,293	41,692	6	9*

* £4,638 less than the previous year.

GROWTH OF THE CHURCH IN LANCASHIRE.

Attention was drawn in the Quarterly Paper No. LXX , for January, 1864, to a paper by the Rev. James Bardsley, on " The Growth of the Church in Lancashire," during the present century. In that county the population had been increasing in an unparalleled manner. The Society had materially contributed to provide increased religious accommodation in that county, where its operations commenced. The existing grants in Lancashire were 75 for curates and 45 for lay agents, benefiting a population of 765,309, at a cost to the Society of 9,210*l.*

AID IN PRINCIPAL DIOCESES.

The Committee also gave in this Paper the following comparative view of the aid rendered by the

Society in some of the principal Dioceses for the last twenty years :—

Diocese		No. of Grants	Grants		Population benefited	Cost to Society.		
			Curates	Lay-agents				
						£	s.	d.
London ...	1843	14	10	4	102,707	1,130	0	0
	1853	26	14	12	178,130	2,200	0	0
	1863	53	34	19	405,780	4,320	0	0
Winchester	1843	12	9	3	104,722	960	0	0
	1853	26	22	4	184,222	1,983	0	0
	1863	38	38	10	254,514	2,925	0	0
Manchester	1843	Formed part of Diocese of Chester.						
	1853	71	44	27	365,065	5,540	0	0
	1863	76	46	30	425,530	5,740	0	0
Chester ...	1843	68	65	3	477,069	5,730	0	0
	1853	73	52	21	412,214	5,895	0	0
	1863	71	47	24	461,838	5,515	0	0
Ripon	1843	49	44	5	345,667	3,865	0	0
	1853	54	45	9	293,728	4,403	0	0
	1863	57	47	10	325,554	4,585	0	0
Worcester	1843	13	8	5	89,430	925	0	0
	1853	39	19	20	222,000	3,020	0	0
	1863	37	27	10	299,777	3,860	0	0

CHARTISM AND INFIDELITY.

On the subject of Chartism and Infidelity the Committee observed that practical infidelity, which manifested itself in the habitual neglect of all religion, abounded to an alarming extent throughout the country, but the general impression was that the working classes were not so largely imbued as they once were with daring infidel and secularist opinions.

The following table showed the number of curates and lay assistants supported by the Society in the Metropolis, and some of the large commercial towns to which grants were made :—

	Curates	Lay-agents	Population benefited	Cost to Society.
				£
London (within Metropolitan circle)	55	20	600,000	6,235
Birmingham	20	18	233,000	3,120
Liverpool	17	10	220,000	2,170
Manchester.........	13	19	188,800	2,365
Bristol......	11	2	76,200	1,090
Sheffield	9	4	92,000	1,080
Bradford............	9	4	66,000	1,040
Halifax	8	2	58,200	765
Leeds	7	1	47,000	695
Nottingham	6	2	57,500	675

THE POTTERIES.

The Quarterly Paper No. LXXI., for April,
1864, contained a wood engraving, "*Iron Miners in
their working dress, with candlesticks in their mouths.*"
The Committee directed attention, in this number,
to that part of Staffordshire called " *The Potteries,*"
included within the Parliamentary Borough of
Stoke-upon-Trent. In 1837 the Society first rendered assistance to this district ; one grant had
been in operation ever since, and at intervals
assistance had been rendered to other districts.
In 1864, stipends for four curates were provided
at a cost to the Society of 400*l.*, benefiting a population of 31,000.

FOREST OF DEAN.

With reference to " *The Forest of Dean,*" the
Committee stated that the border parishes of
Mitcheldean and Newland were those to which
the miners and colliers of the Forest were originally considered to belong, but they were very
seldom seen at church, for the lives and conversation of the majority were most deplorable.
About the year 1812 efforts were made to impart
religious instruction to them, and the clergy of
the adjoining parishes erected a building for the
purposes of Divine worship and education. In
1817 Trinity Church was erected in the north-east
portion of the Forest : this was the first which the

inhabitants could call their own......There were
now five churches in the Forest, and a strong appeal
had lately been put forth by the "Dean Forest
Church Extension Committee" for the building
of three more on the east, south, and west
sides.

The first grant of the Society was made in 1843,
to that portion of the Forest where the *first*
church was built.

THIRTIETH ANNIVERSARY.

The Thirtieth Annual Meeting of the Society
was held in St. James's Hall, Piccadilly, London,
on Thursday, May 4th, 1865, the Earl of Shaftesbury, K.G., in the chair. The speakers were the
Bishops of Carlisle, Ripon, and Winchester; the
Revs. T. R. Birks, J. MacCartie, and S. Thornton;
Sir T. Fowell Buxton, Bart., and Mr. Richard
Hoare. The sermon was preached in St. Dunstan's Church, Fleet Street, London, on the 3rd
of May, 1865, by the Rev. Archibald Boyd, M.A.,
Hon. Canon of Gloucester and Incumbent of Paddington, upon the text 2 Cor. iv. 2.

BISHOP OF WINCHESTER'S FUND.

The Committee in their Report called attention
to the movement commenced by the Bishop of
Winchester in aid of the crowded parishes on the
Surrey side of the Thames.

ENDOWMENT OF BENEFICES—STIPENDS OF CURATES.

The Report stated that the incomes of several
of the incumbents aided by the Society had been
augmented by the Ecclesiastical Commissioners.
It was a cause for much thankfulness that so many
of these benefices, which were miserably small in
point of value, had been thus increased. Nevertheless, the average income of all the incumbents
aided by the Society still came far short of 300*l.*
a-year.

To the important question of the *Stipends of
Curates* the Committee had given their careful
consideration. That the present rate was too low
they felt assured, and therefore it was but just
that some plan should be adopted for increasing
the stipends of curates. But, while recognizing
this in the most distinct manner, they thought that
they should not be justified, except in very special
cases—such as districts entirely destitute—in
making any grant beyond the amount of 100*l.*
Indeed, this could not be done without materially
contracting the Society's operations, unless
resources far larger than they could at present
look for were supplied. They did think, however,
that in voting aid they might, according to the
circumstances of the parish, fairly require, either
from local resources or from those of the benefice,
an addition to the grant, so as to make up a

K

stipend of at least 120*l.* or 130*l.* for curates who had remained a certain time in the same cure; and they believed that there were few instances in which incumbents would be unable to raise the amount required to secure to their parishes the services of a fellow-labourer.

LARGELY INCREASED FUNDS—MRS. SCOTT'S LEGACY.

· The total receipts of the Society in this year amounted to 60,288*l.* 3*s.* 0*d*, being 15,742*l.* 2*s.* 7*d.* more than those of the preceding year. Of this large increase no less than 21,048*l.* 5*s.* 8*d.* arose from legacies, including the gift of the late Mrs. Scott, of Bromley, which amounted to 13,582*l.* 6*s.* 4*d.* consols and cash 380*l.* 18*s.* 4*d.*, making a net value of 12,469*l.* 4*s.* 1*d.* In the year 1847 Mr. Scott's legacy was received, and the Committee appropriated a portion only of that money towards the available income of the Society, and invested the remainder in Long Annuities, terminating in 1860. . . . A somewhat similar course was adopted with the amount received from Mrs. Scott's trustees, which was invested, and the interest thereof, together with a portion of the capital sum, applied annually, so as to sustain for at least ten years about *twenty* additional grants to be called "*the Scott Grants.*"

BISHOP OF LONDON'S FUND—THE SCOTT GRANTS.

· The Executive Committee of this Fund, con-

sidering that it would economise expenditure in
the administration of their Fund . . . voted
1,000*l.* to the Church Pastoral-Aid Society, to be
expended in supplying curates in the poor and
populous parishes of the diocese, additional to
those already provided by the Society in London.
Eight grants of this description were made, and
it was expected that shortly the entire amount
would be appropriated to other necessitous districts.

Besides these "*Block Grants,*" as they were
termed, four other grants for curates and two for
lay agents were also made out of the "Bishop of
London's Fund" to Incumbents who wished the
aid to come through the Church Pastoral-Aid
Society. As the assistance rendered by "*The
Fund*" was only partial, the Committee of the
Society supplemented four of these grants so as
to make up adequate stipends.

The aid of the Society, including the "*Scott*"
and the "*Bishop of London's Fund*" grants, was
at this time afforded to 505 incumbents, in charge
of an aggregate population which gave 7,600 souls
to each. The average income of these incumbents
was 240*l.* per annum, and 202 of them were without parsonage-houses.

FREE AND OPEN CHURCHES.

With regard to the question of "*Free and Open*
K 2

Churches," the Committee stated that in more than
180 of the churches to which the Society made
grants there were no pew-rents whatever, and in
many others only to a small extent. While in
favour of as large a proportion as possible of free
sittings, the Committee felt that unless there was
an adequate endowment, pew-rents were necessary
for the support of the minister.

The Quarterly Paper No. LXXIII., for January,
1865, gave some interesting results of aid in the
southern part of Staffordshire.

EVIL OF STRIKES.

With regard to the evil of the recent "strikes"
amongst the colliers in that district, the Committee
expressed their belief that if our operatives were
properly educated they would not resort to the
custom of "strikes" to settle disputes with their
employers.

THIRTY-FIRST ANNIVERSARY.

The Thirty-first Annual Meeting was held in
St. James's Hall, London, on Thursday, 3rd of
May, 1866, the Earl of Shaftesbury, K.G., in the
chair. The speakers were the Bishop of Peterborough, Archdeacon Prest, the Revs. J. Griffiths
and J. Patteson, Lord Charles Russell, Messrs.
Robert Hanbury, M.P., and Benjamin Shaw. The
sermon was preached in St. Dunstan's Church,
Fleet Street, London, by the Rev. Thomas Sale,

D.D., Hon. Canon of York and Vicar of Sheffield, upon the text Isaiah lix. 19.

ANNUAL INCOME AND GRANTS OF SOCIETY FROM 1836 TO 1866.

The Report contained the following Tabular View of the Annual Income and Grants of the Society :—

Year	Income	Number of Grants		Total Grants	Population benefited
		Curates	Lay-agents		
1836	£ 7,363	58	13	71	542,865
1846	22,505	246	48	294	1,838,741
1856	37,264	343	146	489	2,956,817
1866	42,240	468	165	633	4,000,000 nearly

The amount of funds raised during the first decade of the Society's existence was 162,947*l.* 5*s.* 7*d.* ; in the second period, 343,306*l.* 11*s.* 4*d.* ; and during the third decade it amounted to 443,148*l.* 5*s.* 10*d.* ; making a total of 949,402*l.* 2*s.* 9*d.* The annual average of funds during the first ten years was 16,294*l.* 14*s.* 6*d.* ; in the second 34,330*l.* 13*s.* 1*d.* ; and in the third, 44,314*l.* 16*s.* 7*d.*

AID TO WALES—THE BILINGUAL DIFFICULTY.

Wales was regarded as a most important part of

the Society's sphere of operations. The benefices were generally of small value, and the use of two languages tended to increase the difficulties of the case, for the ministerial duties of the clergy were doubled in performing the requisite services for both English and Welsh parishioners. The following tabular statement of the Society's work in the Principality appeared in the Report :—

	Curates	Lay-agents	Cost to the Society	Population benefited
1836	5	0	240	43,000
1846	19	1	1,532	132,546
1856	31	9	3,085	268,490
1866	63	9	5,330	424,845

The decease of three members of the Committee during the year was recorded, viz., of the Revs. J. Hambleton, T. R. Redwar, and Hugh Stowell; and Messrs. J. R. MacInnes and George Simpson. The Committee announced that the name of the Bishop of Chester had been added to the list of Vice-Patrons of the Society.

ASSOCIATION PROCEEDINGS.

The Rev. W. Kendall having been presented to the incumbency of a new church at Stafford,

retired from the Secretaryship of the North Midland District. The Rev. R. R. Cousens, Incumbent of New Buckenham, Norfolk, was appointed
to succeed the Rev. C. H. Miller as Association Secretary of the South-Eastern or Home
District.

BISHOP OF LONDON'S FUND AND FINANCIAL STATE-MENT OF SOCIETY.

The customary Financial Statement of the
Society did not include the Bishop of London's
Fund.

SCOTT LEGACY.

With regard to "*the Scott Gift*" the Committee
stated that, after much consideration on the subject, they had determined to purchase with it a
Government annuity, yielding 1,476*l.* per annum
for ten years. Twenty additional grants, princi-
pally for curates in charge of districts, had been
made, and would be supported by this annuity
during that period.

STIPENDS OF CURATES.

The Committee, in the Quarterly Paper No.
LXXV., for October, 1865, alluded to the various
plans proposed for increasing the stipends of
curates. Mr. Richard Hoare, at the Anniversary
Meeting, thus expressed the views of the Committee on this question. He said:—"*It is a subject on which we feel deeply. We believe, however,*

that it would be highly improper for us to curtail our
operations, and to limit our sphere of usefulness, by
increasing the salaries of curates ; we feel that if
this is to be done at all, it must be by drawing out
local efforts, and that, when we make a grant to a
parish, we must call upon that parish to supplement
the grant, and thus secure an adequate remuneration
to him who has to labour among the people. Hitherto
our rule has almost invariably been to make no grant
larger than 100l. a year, and we feel that this must
still be maintained ; but I think I may say it is the
feeling of the Committee that in rare and exceptional
cases, they may venture to go beyond that specified
amount." The Bishop of Winchester gave it as
his opinion and the result of much experience,
that it would be highly desirable that the stipend
of curates should be larger than the 100l. a year.
His Lordship referred to the many evils and in-
conveniences arising from inadequate stipends.

Several incumbents applied for an addition of
20l. or 30l. to their existing grants of 100l., not
merely for the purpose of inducing curates to continue in their parishes, but of attracting suitable
men to engage in the work of the ministry in their
large and populous districts. The Committee,
after again giving the entire question their mature
deliberation, drew up the following Resolutions :—

1. "*It is most desirable that the influence of the*
Committee should be exercised in securing to an

efficient curate, remaining two full years in the same parish, among large and poor populations, an increase of stipend."

2. *"That, while the finances and operations of the Society will not admit of any measure for raising the stipends of curates generally out of the funds of the Society, the Committee believe that this great end can, to a considerable extent, be effected by requiring, either from local resources or from those of the benefice, an addition to the grant. And they are confirmed in this opinion by knowing that many incumbents, receiving grants from the Society, have taken steps to increase the salaries of those curates whom they wished to retain."*

3. *"The Committee feel that, except in very special cases, to be considered on their respective merits, they would not be justified in making any grant beyond 100l.; and this in no instance unless to a curate who has been ministering for at least two years in the same parish, and whom the incumbent is anxious to retain, but cannot possibly procure the necessary local resources."*

The Rev. Dr. Miller, in a speech delivered at the Annual Meeting in 1858, observed:—*"I do not hesitate to say that the very least income which a curate in Birmingham, or Manchester, or Liverpool, ought to receive is 150l. a year, and I know men with six children who can hardly get 100l."*

The Earl of Shaftesbury, K.G., in the course of

his speech at the Annual Meeting in 1860, expressed his views on this subject as follows:—
"*Our clergy should be a married clergy. I wish.
that every clergyman were married and had the
means of properly maintaining his wife and family
.........A married clergy is indispensable for a Protestant Church. I cannot find fault with those who,
either by their own judgment or by the judgment of
their parents, decline to enter into holy orders, when
they have less hope than ever of obtaining that support in the Church which will enable them to fill the
station of parochial ministers with dignity and
comfort.*"

The Committee, in the Quarterly Paper No.
LXXVII., for April, 1866, pressed the claims
which the Society had upon all connected with
Liverpool.

TEETOTAL ADVOCACY.

With reference to the subject of "*Teetotalism*"
the Committee directed attention in this Paper to
the following statement of one of the Society's
grantees :—"*The advocates of teetotalism are, unwit-
tingly it may be, but nevertheless surely, doing much
to frustrate and hinder the progress of vital godli-
ness, by holding their meetings on Sundays during
the hours of Divine service and encouraging both old
and young to attend them, to the neglect of the house of
God......I cannot shut my eyes to the fact that the
language of (teetotal) advocates, and the modes*

adopted for gaining proselytes to its ranks, have been, and are still, doing much injury to the cause of true religion."

The Thirty-second Annual Meeting was held in St. James's Hall, London, on Thursday, May 2nd, 1867, the Earl of Shaftesbury, K.G., in the chair. The speakers were the Bishop of Nelson, the Revs. Canon Clayton, W. McCall, W. Mitton, J. C. Ryle, and Dr. Wilkinson, Messrs. Joseph Hoare and Abel Smith, M.P.

The Report alluded to the spread of what was known as "*Ritualism*" in the Church of England as an evil more to be feared than the aggressive movements of the Papacy. The Committee "deprecated needless controversy, but truth must be upheld at every cost."

Infidel teaching amongst the working classes was a question of most serious moment. The employment of lay agency, it was stated, had proved a most effective means of counteracting the progress of infidelity amongst our large populations.

The evils arising from drunkenness were patent to all. The Committee expressed the hope that the Legislature would "speedily amend, if not wholly repeal, the Beerhouse Act, and that steps would also be taken to restrict the sale of intoxicating liquors on the Sabbath."

ASSOCIATION PROCEEDINGS.

The Rev. R. Waters having accepted an incumbency, resigned the Association Secretaryship of the northern district. The Rev. Fielding F. Ould was appointed his successor.

RESERVE FUND.

Mr. J. Bockett expressed his desire " to transfer to trustees, for the use of the Society, 5,000*l.* Stock New Three per Cents., to form the nucleus of a Reserve Fund; the principal to be resorted to only in a case of special emergency and to be replaced as soon as adequate funds shall come in." The Committee fervently hoped that others possessing the ability might be stirred up " to go and do likewise."

The wish of this donor was that the amount should be invested in his own name, and those of two members of the Committee, and the interest only to be used during his lifetime; while placing no restriction on the disposal of the principal after his death, his great desire was that there should be a reserve fund, on which, in seasons of difficulty the Committee might draw.

MACCLESFIELD AND OLDHAM.

The Quarterly Paper No. LXXVIII., for October, 1866, gave many statistics of the Society's work in Macclesfield and Oldham. The evils of the licensing system were enlarged upon in this paper and numerous statistics thereon given. The sanitary condition of the labouring classes was specially alluded to, and it was hoped that public attention would be drawn to those permanent evils which tended to engender epidemic diseases and which were not to be cured by temporary expedients.

MANSION HOUSE RELIEF FUND.

With regard to the several Relief Committees which had been lately called into existence the Report of the Mansion House Committee stated that upwards of 70,000*l.* had been contributed to relieve the sufferers.

The past year had been a remarkable one. A grievous murrain afflicted our herds and flocks, certain localities suffered severely from typhus fever among adults, and scarlatina amongst children, and the cholera also reached our shores.

THIRTY-THIRD ANNIVERSARY.

The Thirty-third Annual Meeting was held in St. James's Hall, London, on Thursday, 7th of May, 1868, the Earl of Shaftesbury, K.G., in the chair. The speakers were the Bishops of Cork and Ripon; the Revs. Canons Brooke and Miller, J. Patteson, J. Richardson, and Sir Willoughby Jones and Mr. Richard Hoare.

The Report contained the following tabular

statement of the populations of parishes aided by
the Society :—

Population 20,000 and upwards	15,000 and under 20,000	10,000 and under 15,000	5,000 and under 10,000	Under 5,000	Total No. of parishes aided
18	23	99	269	139	548

From these figures it would be seen that there
were on the Society's list no fewer than 140
parishes with populations of 10,000 and upwards,
the average being 12,630.

WORK OF ECCLESIASTICAL COMMISSIONERS.

Attention was called to the twentieth Report of
the Ecclesiastical Commissioners for England.
It was remarked that, in this year, the Commissioners would have completed the scheme which,
in their Report of 1864, they proposed to accomplish within five years; every living, therefore,
which then existed with a less income than 300*l.*
a year, and contained, according to the Census of
1861, a population of 4,000, would, on the 1st of
March, 1869, have its income raised to 300*l.* a
year, except those cases in private patronage where
the one-half of the augmentation which the
patrons were required to provide from non-eccle-
siastical sources had not been forthcoming.

FACTORY ACT.

The Committee observed that the extension of this Act to all trades and occupations was joyfully hailed by every friend of the labouring classes. Its main feature was that, all children under a certain age, who laboured at any handicraft, should have secured to them a certain number of hours of schooling every week.

SUNDAY LIQUOR TRAFFIC.

The Committee remarked that, " although the Legislature had not fully adopted the object of the Bill, which provided that all public-houses in England and Wales should be closed on the Sundays, so far as drinking on the premises was concerned, but opened for the sale of liquors over the counter during certain specified periods in the afternoon and evening of the day, still it was encouraging to mark the general and increasing interest taken in this important question.

The Committee announced the decease of the Rev. I. Hughes, Association Secretary for Wales. The Rev. J. Cunnick was appointed to succeed him.

ASSOCIATION ARRANGEMENTS.

The Rev. A. A. Nunn resigned the office of Organizing Secretary in Lancashire. As the Committee felt that the South-eastern or Home district required the full time and strength of any officer, they thought it desirable to terminate the

engagement with the Rev. W. R. Redknap, of
Ryde, the only other clergyman who filled a
similar office. The existing Association arrangements would shortly be reviewed.

LEGACIES—RESERVE FUND.

No less than 16,562l. 2s. 9d. was this year
derived from legacies,* which, with one exception,
was the largest amount ever received; of this
sum 8,000l. was bequeathed by the late Miss
Erskine, of Edinburgh. The Committee thought
it right to transfer 5,000l. of the total amount
received from this source to the Trustees of the
Contingency Fund. The wish of the promoter
of this Fund was that others might be stirred up
to contribute towards a *reserve* on which to fall
back in seasons of financial difficulty, and the
Committee felt that when, as on the present occasion, the legacy receipts were more than usually
large, a certain proportion should be applied to
the same purpose. The annual interest of the
investment would be most useful, and when the
current receipts were contracted the Committee
would not feel the same difficulty as heretofore in
responding to urgent appeals.

The Quarterly Paper No. LXXXI., for October,
1867, contained woodcuts, "*Llanfechan Church*

* The Committee a few years previously characterized this
an uncertain source of income.

restored" and "*Llanfechan old Church*," with results of aid in that district. The remainder of this paper dwelt chiefly on the value and usefulness of the Society in furnishing the means of supporting nearly 500 additional clergy, and of associating them with men of Evangelical senti ments in all parts of the country, especially in our great manufacturing towns and centres.

The Committee stated in the Quarterly Paper No. LXXXII., for January, 1868, that since the Society's formation in 1836, no fewer than *sixteen hundred and sixty-one grants* for the support of clergymen and lay agents had been made; *two hundred and seventy-one* churches had, through its instrumentality, been erected; and there were *two hundred and forty-seven* rooms licensed for Divine Service : most of which would soon lead to more permanent structures.

The Committee directed special attention in this paper to the subject of "*Cottage Hospitals*," in connection with a valuable paper by Dr. Waring. They also quoted approvingly from the recent charge of the Bishop of Ripon on Romanizing tendencies within the Church.

The Quarterly Paper No. LXXXIII., for April, 1868, contained a lengthy quotation from the speech of the Archbishop of York, delivered at the anniversary meeting of the York Auxiliary.

L

THIRTY-FOURTH ANNIVERSARY.

The Thirty-fourth Annual Meeting was held in St. James's Hall, London, on Thursday, May 6th, 1869, the Earl of Shaftesbury, K.G., in the Chair. The speakers were the Revs. James Bardsley, C. Kemble, J. H. Titcomb, T. Walters, S. Winter; and Messrs. Arthur Mills and B. Shaw. The sermon was preached in St. Dunstan's Church, Fleet Street, London, on the 5th of May, 1869, by Bishop Ryan, upon the text 1 Peter v. 2.

THE SUNDAY QUESTION.

The Report contained the following observation upon "*The Sunday Question*":—"It is encouraging to know that whilst there are many who are associated together to destroy the religious sanctity and public observance of the Christian Sabbath, the voice of the working classes generally had been very emphatically expressed with regard to this proposition."

Touching upon the work of the Ecclesiastical Commission, the Committee observed that incumbents labouring among *mining populations* might obtain from the Ecclesiastical Commissioners partial stipends for curates, and that several of these incumbents had applied to the Society for the residue. *Thirty-eight* grants of this character had been made.

The augmentation of the incomes of poor benefices had been a most important work. In 1840 the average incomes of parishes aided by the Society was only 161*l.*; in 1850 it was 199*l.*; in 1860, 210*l.*; and in 1869 it reached 270*l.*

The Committee recorded the decease of the Archbishop of Canterbury and the Bishop of Peterborough, Vice-Patrons of the Society. The name of the Bishop of Peterborough's successor had been enrolled on their list of Vice-Patrons.

LEGACIES.

The Report stated that but for the extraordinary sum derived from legacies the income would have fallen considerably below the expenditure. What was wanted was a regular income of 50,000*l.*, exclusive of legacies. At this they aimed—for this they pleaded.

FUNDS.

The amount of funds raised during the first decade of the Society's existence was 162,947*l.* 5*s.* 7*d.*; in the second period, 343,306*l.* 11*s.* 4*d.*; in the third decade, 443,148*l.* 5*s.* 10*d.* : making a total of 949,402*l.* 2*s.* 9*d.*

The *annual average of Funds* during the first ten years was 16,294*l.* 14*s.* 6*d.*; in the second, 34,330*l.* 13*s.* 1*d.*; and in the third, 44,314*l.* 16*s.* 7*d.*

The Quarterly Paper No. LXXXIV., for October,.

ECCLESIASTICAL COMMISSIONERS.

1868, sketched the effects of " *The New Prefer-
ment Act* " of 1837. It was stated that " the Ecclesiastical Commissioners had increased to 300*l.*
a-year all livings with populations above 4,000.
Besides this, they had offered to meet with grants
of an equal amount augmentations from private
sources, providing one-half the amount necessary
to raise to 300*l.* a-year the income of any such
livings in *private patronage.*" It was to be hoped
that further resources would in due time be at the
command of the Ecclesiastical Commissioners, so
as to enable them to extend aid to numerous
parishes below the limit now reached, and which
stood in great need of assistance.

The Quarterly Paper No. LXXXVI., for April,
1869, gave statistics of the growth of the population of England and Wales since the year 1377.

THIRTY-FIFTH ANNIVERSARY.

The Thirty-fifth Annual Meeting was held in
St. James's Hall, London, on Thursday, May 5th,
1870, the Earl of Shaftesbury, K.G., in the chair.
The speakers were the Bishop of Ripon and the
Dean of Ripon, the Revs. J. Blomefield, W. Cadman, T. M. Macdonald, and Messrs. P. O'Malley,
Q.C., and P. V. Smith. The Sermon was preached
in St. Dunstan's Church, Fleet Street, London, on
the 1st of May, 1870, by the Bishop of London,
upon the text Acts xx. 20.

ELEMENTARY EDUCATION.

On the subject of Elementary Education the Report stated that it was but fifty-eight years since the National Society was founded, and thirty-eight years since the Educational Committee of the Privy Council was formed. The results achieved by our voluntary system were little short, as the Report of the Royal Commission on Education in 1858 showed, of those attained by the Prussian compulsory system. It was to be hoped that the legislative measure adopted would be for the *extension of the present system, with such additions as our increased population rendered necessary to complete the education of the poorer classes.*

PAROCHIAL MAGAZINE ASSOCIATIONS.

Under the head of " *Parochial Magazine Associations* " the Committee referred to the importance of the establishment of magazine and book depôts for the sale of periodicals of a moral and elevating character.

The Committee announced that the names of the Bishops of Winchester, Bath and Wells, Carlisle, and St. Asaph had been added to the list of Vice-Patrons.

The Committee, in the Quarterly Paper No. LXXXVII., for October, 1869, drew attention to the subject of a book termed "*Underground Life; or, Mines and Miners,*" by L. Simonin, as one of national interest, and alluded to the appalling catastrophes at the Hartley Pit, Ferndale, and Brierley Hill. It was computed that 300,000 persons were annually employed in the coal mines of Great Britain. The Society granted aid largely in the mining and colliery districts.

The same paper gave various statistics published by the National Society, and stated that out of 14,700 ecclesiastical parishes or districts in England and Wales, 12,000 had separate week-day schools under Church management. It was not to be inferred that the remainder were without education, as in many towns large central schools had been established, which served for several adjoining parishes, and in these cases the parishes were returned as without schools of their own. It appeared that only forty-two per cent. of Church of England week-day schools were aided by the Committee of Council; but these were the largest schools, and fifty-nine per cent. of the scholars were in inspected schools.

The Quarterly Paper No. LXXXVIII., for January, 1870, stated that there were on the books of the Society thirteen parishes, with a population of 20,000 and upwards; *twenty* parishes, from 15,000 to 20,000; and *one hundred and three*, with populations from 10,000 to 15,000. In most of these the work of *sub-division* was going forward.

The Quarterly Paper No. LXXXIX., for April,

1870, treated of the Bilingual difficulty, which, it was observed, was probably the greatest of those with which the Church in Wales had to contend. In at least one half of the 1,045 parishes or ecclesiastical districts into which the Principality is divided, it was a condition necessary to success that the clergyman be acquainted with both languages, but his Welsh " should be very good, and not that foreign-taught or thinking in English language which is so often heard in the Welsh pulpits of the Church." That the Society was seeking to remedy this special difficulty in the Principality would be seen from the following table, showing the comparative

INCREASE OF GRANTS IN THE PRINCIPALITY DURING THE
LAST THIRTY YEARS.

	Parishes aided	Grants for		Total grants	Population benefited	Cost to the Society	Amount received from the Principality
		Curates	Lay agents				
						£	£
1840	14	17	...	17	89,800	1,335	414
1850	19	20	5	25	235,555	1,980	433
1860	35	40	7	47	307,437	3,560	1,178
1870	71	81	10	91	447,477	5,728	1,296

SUMMARY OF GRANTS ACCORDING TO WELSH DIOCESES.

	No. of Incumbents	Population	No. of grants		Cost to the Society	Amount to meet Grants	Churches	Licensed rooms	Additional Services			
			Curates	Lay agents					Lord's day	Week-day	Cottage Lectures	Bible-classes
St. Asaph	6	29,450	6	...	£ 415	£ 295	0	4	9	6	4	4
Bangor ...	8	31,296	8	2	640	400	4	9	16	9	8	12
St. David's	24	132,610	31	1	2,170	1,190	12	18	59	31	32	21
Llandaff ...	33	254,121	36	7	2,503	1,580	11	22	58	38	33	44
	71	447,477	81	10	5,728	3,465*	27	53	142	84	77	81

Attempts had been made in various ways to meet the Bilingual difficulty. English clergymen had studied for a time the Welsh language, and, after acquiring a little knowledge of it, had been instituted to benefices in the Principality; but this system had been regarded as a complete failure. The clergy, as a rule, must be thoroughly Welshmen, fully knowing and sympathizing with the Welsh national characteristics, especially

* Of this amount 2,940l. is derived from the Ecclesiastical Commissioners.

the Celtic temperament. The Welsh bishops, through the dearth of proper candidates for the ministry, had been obliged to admit into holy orders some who were ready speakers in their native tongue, but from want of early education were sadly deficient in English. *While these were adapted for one portion* of our population, they were not qualified to minister to the other.

The Thirty-sixth Annual Meeting was held in St. James's Hall, London, on Thursday, May 4th, 1871, the Earl of Shaftesbury, K.G., in the chair. The speakers were the Revs. Joseph Bardsley, F. S. Cook, W. A. Cornwall, Dr. Griffiths ; and Messrs. Hugh Birley, M.P., and Samuel Hoare. The sermon was preached in St. Dunstan's Church, Fleet Street, London, on Wednesday, the 3rd of May, 1871, by the Dean of Canterbury, upon the text 2 Tim. iv. 2.

The Quarterly Paper No. XC., for October, 1870, contained a " *Map of England and Wales, showing the six districts of the Association Secretaries of the Church Pastoral-Aid Society*" and various reports of the Association Secretaries. It was remarked that " if many of the clergy could be prevailed upon to act as honorary secretaries, and make within a small circle around 'their' respective parishes the necessary arrangements for sermons and meetings, the income might be easily raised up to the liabilities, and pressing applications for aid could at once be responded to.

The Committee believed that, with some effort of this kind, the number of clerical subscribers, now not more than 2,000, could be considerably increased. A large number of small subscriptions might also be obtained by the zealous efforts of collectors deputed for this special service. They strongly recommended the issue of collecting-boxes under the special management of a person thoroughly interested in the Society's work.

It was stated that during the year 1869 *collecting boxes* realized about 800*l*. If they were more widely circulated, a far larger amount in small sums might be expected.

EXTRACTS FROM QUARTERLY PAPERS.

The Quarterly Paper No. XCI., for January, 1871, drew attention to the depressed state of the funds of the Society. It was stated that some friends thought that a *large* proportion of the amount derived from legacies should be invested as a Reserve Fund, and their impression was that the present embarrassment of the Society arose from not adopting this plan. The Committee remarked that a certain proportion was added to the fund already set aside for that purpose; but the remainder was actually required for the ordinary

payments of the year arising from the past extension of operations.

The Thirty-seventh Annual Meeting was held
in St. James's Hall, London, on Thursday, May
2nd, 1872, the Earl of Shaftesbury, K.G., in the chair.
The speakers were the Bishop of Gloucester and
Bristol, the Revs. Clement Cobb, W. McCall, O.
Phillips, A. W. Snape, Dr. Tyng, and Mr. Gur-
ney Hoare. The sermon was preached in St.
Pancras Parish Church, London, on Sunday morn-
ing, the 28th of April, 1872, by the Bishop of
Ripon, upon the text Romans i. 16.

The Committee stated, in the Quarterly Paper
No. XCIII., for October, 1871, that correspondents referred with great thankfulness to the
result of their "*Mission Services*," and the Special
Meetings for prayer, which were held every evening through the week, and they expressed their
belief, that, without any excitement, there had
been a real and lasting revival of religion.

In their Annual Report they observed that
Tuesday, the 27th of February, was a day which
would long be remembered. On that day of
"National Thanksgiving" for the recovery of the
Prince of Wales men unaccustomed to religious
feeling, bowed under it, and from many a heart
arose deep and sincere gratitude to the Giver of
all blessings. It was no formal demonstration,

but the natural emotion of a great and a free people happy in their institutions, and desiring to record that feeling of happiness in a way which was, in a double sense, a thanksgiving.

On the subject of Elementary Education the Report observed that for the most part the grantees of the Society had urged on their parishioners the advantage of supporting their schools on the present voluntary system, thereby securing the liberty of conducting them on religious principles, and of teaching the children a system of definite religious belief according to the doctrines and principles of the Church of England. Every effort had been used to make the school accommodation in their several districts amply sufficient for the wants of the population. They also felt that if eventually our National Schools should be placed under School Boards the expenses of their management and maintenance would be greatly increased. It was encouraging to know that the School Board of London, as well as other Boards throughout the country, had resolved "That in the schools provided by the Board the Bible shall be read, and there shall be given such explanations and such instructions therefrom in the principles of morality and religion as are suited to the capacities of children." The result of the late education debate in Parliament most satisfactorily proved that the attempts of those who would overthrow existing voluntary schools, and set up an irreligious system of national elementary education, would not be tolerated.

The decease of Mr. John Bockett was announced. He had been, for many years, a most liberal supporter of the Society, and by his gift of 5,000*l*. laid the foundation of a Reserved Fund.

The Thirty-eighth Annual Meeting was held in St. James's Hall, London, on Thursday, May 8th, 1873, the Earl of Shaftesbury, K.G., in the chair. The speakers were Bishop Ryan and the Bishop of Nelson, the Revs. T. F. Fergie, J. Griffith, J. Smith, and G. W. Weldon, and Mr. Benjamin Shaw. The sermon was preached in St. Dunstan's Church, Fleet Street, London, on the 7th of May, 1873, by the Rev. Sir Emilius Bayley, Bart., B.D., Vicar of St. John's, Paddington, London, upon the text Isaiah lxv. 8.

The Report stated that *Mission Services* had been held during the past year in Sheffield, Hull, Birmingham, and other large towns, and the results had been signally blessed. The Committee adverted to the formation of the Church of England Temperance Society, which had been organized under the highest ecclesiastical auspices. Its distinctive feature was, to include all who were willing to take part in an organized effort to reduce the bane of intemperance, whether they were or were not ready to give up their own tastes and habits in the cause.

The decease of Mr. James Farish, an old and much esteemed member of the Committee, was recorded.

In a note appended to the "Statement of Funds" of this year the Committee stated that they had found it convenient to take the whole of the house in Falcon Court, on a short lease, and the House Rent Account represented the rent received from the tenants of the rooms not occupied by the Society.

The Quarterly Paper No. XCVI., for October, 1872, stated that a liberal supporter of the Society, the late Mrs. Fane, proposed to support during her life three additional curates, two in London and one in Liverpool. For the last two or three years the same friend had also paid the stipend of a curate in London, and of a lay-agent in a large provincial town. Encouraged by this proposal, as well as by the liberal contribution of a West-end congregation, the Committee added five to the list of metropolitan grants, making a total of 95—67 for curates, and 28 for lay-agents.

The following table showed what was doing in some of the great centres of industry, and what returns they made to the Society:—

| PLACE. | Population benefited. | Grants for | | Cost to the Society. | Contributions from the respective places to the Society. |
		Curates.	Lay-agents.		
				£	£
Liverpool	284,915	23	7	2,650	1,657
Birmingham ...	279,218	28	21	4,100	1,250
Manchester and Salford	244,144	19	20	2,780	1,704
Sheffield.........	96,045	10	2	1,005	748
Blackburn	94,472	14		1,190	305
Bradford.........	81,955	10	5	1,280	364
Bristol	81,373	15	1	1,360	1,078
Leeds	78,189	7	6	1,030	367
Nottingham ...	69,983	9	3	1,030	593
Hull	61,045	8	3	890	423

The Thirty-ninth Annual Meeting was held in St. James's Hall, London, on Thursday, 7th of May, 1874, the Earl of Shaftesbury, K.G., in the chair. The speakers were the Bishops of Gloucester and Bristol, and St. Asaph; the Revs. Sir Emilius Bayley, Bart., R. C. Billing, Latimer Jones, W. Lefroy, and T. A. Stowell, and Mr. James Bateman. The sermon was preached on the 6th of May, 1874, in St. Dunstan's Church, Fleet Street, London, by the Dean of Chester, upon the words of the Gospel St. John xx. 21, 22, 23.

CENSUS TABLES.

The Committee, alluding in their Report to the

Census Tables, stated that it was not until the first year of the present century that any effective means were adopted for numbering the people of the United Kingdom, and the Census of 1801 fell very far short of that which even then was desired. The facts which were collected at the first English Census seemed most meagre in comparison with the elaborate calculations of 1871. The third volume of the late Census, giving statistics of the ages, civil condition, occupations, and birthplaces of the people, has been speedily followed by the fourth volume, or General Report, which was a kind of Imperial Census. The Committee referred to some particulars of the Census which were more immediately connected with the operations of the Society.

Upon the work of the *Ecclesiastical Commission* the Report observed that the utmost the Commissioners were enabled at present to accomplish in the way of endowing small livings, irrespective of the grants to meet benefactions of an equal amount, was to make up to 300*l.* a year the income of benefices in public patronage having a population of 4,000, and already constituted at the date of the last Census, and also to endow with 200*l.* a year a limited number of new churches having a like population attached to them, and with districts legally assigned since the above date.

The Committee sincerely hoped that the time might speedily come when the Commissioners would be in a position to aid benefices with a population as low even as 2,000. There were many livings with an income much below 200*l.* a year, and though it might fairly be said that in respect of population the claim in such cases was not so strong as in the case of those which now received assistance, still it was well known that, practically speaking, the demand which was made on the time and strength of clergymen labouring among smaller, but often scattered, flocks was almost equally great. It was, therefore, greatly to be desired that such benefices should, as soon as possible, be raised to the improved scale of 300*l.* adopted in the case of larger populations.

The Committee further stated that at one time there were several grants on the Society's list for augmenting the incomes of ill-endowed benefices; but in recent years the Committee had not felt themselves justified in responding to appeals of this character except under exceptional circumstances. At present there were eleven cases only of incumbents whose incomes were furnished, either in whole or in part, by the Society.

SPECIAL MISSIONS.—A Committee on this subject was held on the 14th July, 1874. There were present Mr. W. N. West, in the chair; the Revs. C. F. S. Money, Dr. Nolan, and E. J. Speck (Secretary of the Society).

M

Several letters were read from clergy in different parts of the country expressing their gratification that the Society had taken up the work of Special Missions, and wishing their names to be added to the list. The Secretary stated that he had been in correspondence with the Rev. G. Chute, of Market Drayton, and the Rev. H. Harkness, of Berrow, respecting the missionaries in their parishes, and that he had been able to supply their wants.

Letters were read from the Revs. J. Maughan, J. Whitby, and R. Mills, of Leeds, stating that it was the intention of the clergy of Leeds to institute a Mission in the early part of January next, and applying to the Society for missionaries to visit them at that time.

It was suggested that the Secretary should ask the Revs. A. W. Thorold, E. H. Bickersteth, J. F. Kitto, W. Milton, W. V. Jackson, and others, if a larger number should be necessary, and that the Secretary should name those able to comply with the request to the Leeds Committee of Evangelical Clergy rather than send a list to select from.

Letters were read from the Revs. H. G. Thwaites (Birmingham), J. T. Wrenford (Newport, Mon.), and G. Dobree (Worksop), referring with thankfulness to the permanent results of their respective Missions

The Special Mission Committee met on the 15th of December, 1874. Colonel Channer occupied the chair, and there were present the Revs. R. R. Cousens, Dr. Nolan, and E. J. Speck, Secretary of the Society. The Secretary stated that Special Missions had been arranged at the following places :—

PLACE.	INCUMBENT.	MISSIONER.
West Meon	A. B. Burton	R. R. Cousens
Normanton	W. M. Lane	G. Dobree
Deptford (Sunderland)	G. B. Moffatt......	A. C. Downer
Tunstall..............	R. Hawes	J. R. Starey
Cobridge	J. A. McMullen...	W. W. Tyler

A list was read of Evangelical clergymen who had undertaken to conduct the Leeds Mission in January, 1875. Out of the seventeen churches in that town fourteen missioners had been secured.

It was stated that in November a successful Mission took place in West Meon and the surrounding districts under the Rev. A. B. Burton. The Rev. R. R. Cousens assisted in carrying out the work.

The Secretary announced that a Mission was to be held at Normanton in February next, and that

M 2

the Rev. G. Dobree, of St. John's, Worksop, had promised to undertake it.

Missions were also to be held in many other places, for which the Secretary had provided preachers.

In connection with the subject of *Welsh Missions* the Secretary read a letter from the Rev. J. Griffiths, of Llanllwchaiarn, New Quay, suggesting a few able Welsh clergymen to conduct them. Mr. Griffiths was anxious to hold a Mission in Lent. The Rev. John Griffith, of Neath, was asked to undertake it.

The total sum granted from October, 1874, to March, 1878, towards the expenses of Special Missions was 231*l.* 19*s.* 1*d.*

The Committee stated in the Report for 1874 that many friends of the Society, feeling that the results of the "Missions" held in their respective neighbourhoods had exceeded their most sanguine expectations, and believing that the success vouchsafed was an indication that the work of "Home Missions" would become a recognised agency in our Church, lately urged upon the Committee the importance of obtaining a list of clergymen of Evangelical views ready and qualified to visit any parish where their services might be desired......
The Committee expressed their readiness, so far as they could consistently with the rules and objects of the Society, to adopt the suggestions of

their friends. They were now forming such a list,
and the Secretary would be glad to hear from
those who might be willing to have their names
added to it.

The Committee becoming aware that the
"Church Home and Special Mission" had the
same object in view, a conference between the
Committees of the two Societies was held, when
it was determined that the "Church Home and
Special Mission" should continue its original
work of providing preachers for fortnightly services on certain circuits in the country, but that
the Church Pastoral-Aid Society should take up
the Special Mission work. Some members of the
Committee of the "Church Home and Special
Mission" had agreed to join the Committee of
the Church Pastoral-Aid Society with a view to
aid in the discharge of the duties connected with
this special organization.

It was announced that applications for pecuniary assistance towards any Special Mission
should be made to the Committee before the commencement of the Mission. On receiving such
applications the Committee would be prepared, in
cases approved by them, to make grants in advance, not exceeding 5l., towards the expenses of
the Mission.

The Report went on to state that making every
abatement for some practices which the Society

could not endorse, and admitting, also, that some of the deep interest which was felt in the varied Mission services might prove to have been but temporary and would therefore pass away with the emotional excitement by which they were accompanied, it was nevertheless to be hoped that a real and abiding work had, by God's blessing, been accomplished in awakening numbers of the careless and profane, in confirming the truth in the hearts of His faithful people, and in imparting fresh zeal and life to the ministry of the Gospel of Christ.

That the work of the Society would be more than ever needed was evident, for the fruits of these Missions must be sustained and nourished; and this could only be effectually done by personal intercourse with persons at their own homes.

FUNDS.—The list of donations included the sum of 4,000*l.* received from four sons of the late Mr. Francis Wright, of Osmaston Manor, Derby, " *in memoriam* " of their revered father.

The Committee felt that this liberal contribution should be devoted to some special object, and they therefore invested the amount with a view of applying it to the purchase of a house in which the business of the Society could be permanently carried on.

The following changes with respect to the Asso-

ciation Secretaries were reported :—The Rev.
Fielding Ould, having been appointed to a benefice, was succeeded by the Rev. Dr. Peake, in the
Northern district; the Rev. J. A. Jamieson,
formerly in charge of the North Midland district,
was transferred to the South-Western district, and
was succeeded by the Rev. C. D. Russell.

Shortly after the publication of the Quarterly
Paper No. XCVIII., for April, 1873, the Secretary
received a letter signed "*A Working Man,*"* containing an enclosure of 50*l.* The donor had been
forcibly struck with the number and urgency of
"cases waiting for aid," and wrote as follows:—
"I trust and believe that the Holy Spirit put it into
my mind to offer 50*l.* to the Pastoral-Aid Society
towards raising a sum of 50,000*l.* for the immediate use of the Society. *If only one thousand*
persons should be moved by the same blessed
Spirit to contribute a similar sum, the thing will
be done at once......I do this......with an intense
desire to wipe from the Pastoral-Aid Society's
Paper what I conceive to be a discredit to the
religion of Jesus Christ my blessed Lord and
Master—' Cases Waiting for Aid.' "

Several friends of the Society responded to the
appeal of the "*Working Man,*" and forwarded
cheques of 50*l.* each.

The Committee stated in the Quarterly Paper

* This letter was published in the *Record.*

No. CI., for April, 1874, on the subject of popular
education, that "recent legislative action would
be productive of good results if it awakened a
more earnest attention to the religious education
of the young, and to the great value of Sunday-
schools, not as mere adjuncts to the day-schools,
but as constituting a distinct and independent
agency.   It was evident· that our Sunday-
schools should be brought to the utmost state of
efficiency. As the scholars in our day-schools
were rising to a higher standard of education than
formerly, it became increasingly difficult to secure
qualified teachers on the Sunday."

The Fortieth Annual Meeting was held in St.
James's Hall, London, on Thursday, May 6th,
1875, the Earl of Shaftesbury, K.G., in the chair.
The speakers were the Bishop of Gloucester and
Bristol, and the Revs. Dr. Burges, J. Griffith,
P. S. O'Brien, T. Whitby, and H. Woodward.
The sermon was preached by the Bishop of St.
Asaph, upon the text Acts xxvi. 17, 18.

The Committee called attention in the Quarterly
Paper No. CII., for October, 1874, to a collecting-
box of a novel design, labelled thus :—

THANKOFFERINGS

TO THE

CHURCH PASTORAL-AID SOCIETY

(A Home Missionary Society).

1 Cor. xvi. 2.   2 Chron. xxix. 31.

The title "*Thankofferings*," it was thought,
would remove the objection entertained by some to
collecting-boxes, which were often used as *begging-
boxes*.

FINANCIAL DIFFICULTY.—The Committee announced at the Anniversary Meeting in May,
1874, that the operations of the Society had been
very materially enlarged during the previous year.
Since that time sixty-two new grants had been
made—forty-eight for curates, and fourteen for lay
assistants—involving a cost of 4,945*l*.; but during
the same period twenty-nine grants had lapsed at a
reduction of 2,012*l*., leaving a balance of thirty-
three additional grants, at an annual cost of 2,933*l*.
to the funds of the Society. The receipts were
less at this time by 11,000*l* than at the corresponding period of 1874, but this deficiency was
owing entirely to the very large amount of legacies,
and a special donation of 4,000*l*. received in 1874.
The income of the Society for 1875 could not be
estimated at more than 49,000*l*., and as the then
rate of expenditure was 55,600*l*., and the liabilities (if all the grants were in operation) would
amount to 67,617*l*., it was very evident that a large
addition to the funds of the Society was needed in
order to keep up its operations.

The Report stated that a very successful Mission
took place in Leeds in January, 1875. A corre-
spondent wrote :—" As a memorial of the Mission

in Leeds, it is proposed to raise (and it will be done) 10,000*l.* for church building."

In addition to the ordinary receipts, the Committee announced that they had received from Mrs. Disney Robinson, in memory of her late husband, the sum of 5,000*l.*, which had been invested in the names of trustees, with a view to assist the Society in making five additional grants towards the support of curates in parishes or districts in the West Riding of Yorkshire. These grants had already been made, and the Committee would, out of the General Fund, supply what was necessary to make up the stipends of the five curates.

WANT OF CURATES.

The Report stated that one great and increasing difficulty incumbents had to contend with was the want of curates. The demand for additional clergymen throughout the country had, of late years, very greatly increased on account of the formation of new district-parishes, and the extinction of the evil of pluralities; in consequence of this no fewer than 134 of the Society's grants for curates were at present unoccupied.

The following analysis of ordinations in 1874 was taken from " *The Literary Churchman* ":—

	Deacons.	Priests.	Oxford, Camb., Durham, & Dublin	From Theol. Colls.	Others	Total.
Lent	94	86	129	34	17	180
Trinity	164	170	255	67	12	334
June 28 (Durham)	14	12	18	8	0	26
July 25 (York) ...	12	21	18	11	4	33
September	132	101	168	51	14	233
Advent	223	234	339	93	25	455
Total for the year.	639	624	927	264	72	1,261

The number of deacons ordained in 1873 was
630, so that the advance in the newly ordained
which was observed in that year was well maintained. The *average* of the ten years ending 1873
was 598, and that of the ten preceding years
ending 1863 was 600.

The Forty-first Annual Meeting was held in St.
James's Hall, London, on Thursday, 4th of May,
1876, the Earl of Shaftesbury, K.G., in the chair.
The speakers were the Revs. H. Barne, W.
Cadman, T. D. Halsted, Canon Miller, Parker

Morgan, and the Hon. Thomas Pelham.   The
sermon was preached in St. Dunstan's Church,
Fleet Street, London, on the 3rd of May, 1876,
by the Bishop of Norwich, on the words of the
Gospel St. John xii. 24—26.

The Committee recorded the decease of the
Rev. Joseph Haslegrave, one of the earliest clerical
members of the Committee.

The Bishop of St. David's accepted the office
of a Vice-Patron of the Society.

Allusion was made in the Report to a return of
the Education Department, giving details with
reference to public elementary schools.   The
most striking feature of the return was the
evidence it afforded of the disproportionately large
share of the burden of elementary education
which was borne by the Established Church.   It
contributed, as regarded the number on the rolls,
an average attendance nearly double the amount
of the united provision made by the British
schools and the Roman Catholic and Board
schools.

With regard to church building, the Report
stated that it had been calculated, on good authority, that the total amount expended by Churchmen in the erection and maintenance of
elementary schools between the years 1811 and
1874, amounted to no less than 27,000,000l., and

that of this sum a total of 3,070,962*l.* was contributed during the five years ending in August, 1874. The total sum expended on churches within the last thirty-five years, according to a Parliamentary return, had been no less than 26,000,000*l.* Sums under 500*l.* had been omitted, and would alone amount to a considerable sum.

Supply of Clergy.—The following comparative view, drawn from the Census Returns, conveys a tolerably accurate idea on this subject :—

—	No. of Clergy.	No. of Churches.	No. of lay people to each clergyman.
1841	14,527	13,318	1,095
1851	17,320	14,077	1,035
1861	19,195	14,731	1,045
1871	20,674	15,522	1,097

The difficulty in procuring curates naturally caused many of the Society's grants to be unoccupied. The following statement of the number of those out of operation during the last twenty years is here given :—

Date April 1st.	No. of parishes aided.	Total No. of Grants.		No. of Grants in operation.		No. of Grants out of operation.		Total liability.	Total actual expenditure.
		Curates.	Lay-agents.	Curates.	Lay-agents.	Curates.	Lay-agents.	£	£
1856	389	343	146	311	135	32	11	42,465	38,018
1861	442	400	156	348	143	52	13	48,815	42,627
1866	500	468	165	377	156	91	9	55,280	46,214
1871	600	536	206	434	195	102	11	60,638	53,305
1876	705	623	239	469	214	154	25	70,016	54,824

INTEMPERANCE.

Intemperance the Committee have ever regarded as one of the greatest obstacles to the minister of the Gospel. The Church of England Temperance Society, which included within its ranks not only total abstainers, but also all who recognised the duty of moderation in the use of alcoholic drinks, had been established to impress upon the public mind the conviction that this was not merely a question of social importance, but a great religious question, as the prevalence of this evil brought a scandal on a Christian nation.

COMPARATIVE INCOMES OF THE CHURCH PASTORAL-
AID AND ADDITIONAL CURATES SOCIETIES.

The Committee, in the Quarterly Paper No. CV., for October, 1875, considered that no misapprehension ought to exist as to the comparative extent of the work done by our two principal Home Missionary Societies, and they therefore thought it right to lay before their friends the following correspondence with the Bishop of London. The Bishop having, in a pastoral letter, issued in December of 1874, made no mention whatever of the important operations of the Church Pastoral-Aid Society in the diocese of London, the Committee addressed his Lordship on the subject in the following terms :—

" Temple Chambers, Falcon Court,
" Fleet Street, London, E.C.
" 13th May, 1875.

" MY LORD,—The attention of the Committee of the Church Pastoral-Aid Society has been called to your Lordship's letter, dated 2nd December, 1874, and addressed to the clergy and laity of the diocese of London, in which your Lordship commends especially to their help and sympathy the work and objects of the Additional Curates Society, on the ground of its undertaking to continue the curates' stipends hitherto provided by the Bishop of London's Fund. The Committee beg to remind your Lordship that upon the Bishop of London's Fund ceasing to contribute to the stipends of parochial curates, the Church Pastoral-Aid Society, no less than

the Additional Curates Society, undertook to continue
out of its own funds the stipends of curates which were
previously paid through its agency by the Bishop of London's Fund.

" But your Lordship proceeds to mention the aggregate
number of curates (whether transferred from the books
of the Bishop of London's Fund or not) supported by the
Additional Curates Society in the diocese of London,
and to rest the claims of that Society on the fact of its
making no fewer than sixty-eight grants in the diocese of
London to parishes containing an aggregate population
of 628,000 souls.   Your Lordship adds, ' During last
year no less than 7,863*l*. (including the sums locally
raised to meet the grants) was guaranteed through the
agency of the Additional Curates Society for the
stipends of additional curates in our diocese ; while, on
the other hand, the whole sum raised throughout the
diocese of London by church collections and offertories
for the Society's General Fund amounted only to 1,100*l*.'

" The Committee desire me to point out to your Lordship that the Church Pastoral-Aid Society is entitled,
upon similar grounds, to the sympathy and support of
Churchmen in the diocese of London.   It at present
makes seventy-eight grants in the diocese, at a total cost
(including the sums raised from local or other sources to
meet the grants) of 7,541*l*., and benefiting, in all, a population of 524,296 souls.   Of the seventy-eight grants,
forty-nine are for curates and twenty-nine for lay
assistants, the aggregate stipends of the former being
5,456*l*., and the latter 2,085*l*.   Of these amounts the sums
of 4,410*l*. and 2,055*l*. respectively are paid out of the
General Fund of the Society.

" Within the whole area comprised in the Metropolitan Circle, the Church Pastoral-Aid Society makes

no fewer than one hundred and sixteen grants, seventy-six of which are for curates and forty for lay assistants. The aggregate population thus benefited amounts to 849,589 souls, and the total cost to the General Fund of the Society (exclusive of sums raised locally to meet the grants) is 9,657*l.*

"The Committee feel assured that these facts could not have been brought under your Lordship's notice when you wrote a letter of the 2nd of December, 1874, or your Lordship (being one of the Vice-Patrons of the Church Pastoral-Aid Society) would not have failed to commend that Society jointly with the Additional Curates Society to the help and sympathy of the clergy and laity of the diocese of London. They are confident, however, that the supply of the foregoing information will procure from your Lordship a public recognition of the strong claims of the Church Pastoral-Aid Society upon the diocese, similar to the acknowledgment which you have made of the work done in London by the younger Society.

"I have the honour to be, my Lord,
"Your Lordship's obedient servant,
(Signed) "EDWARD J. SPECK,
"Secretary.
"The Right Hon. and Right Rev. the
Lord Bishop of London."

To this communication the Bishop sent the following reply, with full permission for its publication :—

"Fulham Place, S.W., May 17th, 1875.

"DEAR SIR,—I can assure the Committee of the Church Pastoral-Aid Society that I have never been unmindful of the good work the Society has done and is doing in the diocese of London.

N

" When, on the reconstitution of the Bishop of London's Fund, the Board found it necessary to omit from the list of its objects the supply of parochial curates (as distinct from missionary clergy), and consequently to withdraw their grants from the two Societies through whose agency their curate grants had for the most part been made, the Additional Curates Society represented to me that they were able to continue from their own funds the stipends which had been paid out of the Bishop of London's grant, only on condition that I gave them last autumn a circular letter to the public. This I consented to do, and I should have been ready, and am still ready, to do the same for the Pastoral-Aid Society, if thought desirable. I did not volunteer it, because such appeals, if not necessary, are inexpedient, and become less effective each time they are repeated. I shall, however, be very glad to do what I can to further the interests and usefulness of the Society, if the Committee will, after consideration, furnish me with their views and wishes.

" I am, dear Sir, faithfully yours,
(Signed)   " J. LONDON.

"Rev. E. J. Speck."

The Committee took this opportunity of correcting a misapprehension respecting the comparative incomes of the two Societies. The Additional Curates Society included in its income the sums raised locally to meet its grants. In the Report for the year ending December, 1873, the total income of the Society was stated as 55,270*l.*, but of this amount 24,867*l.* were remittances, under Rule 6, " For the specific purpose of supplying the spiritual wants of a particular parish or district." If the same course were adopted by the Church Pastoral-Aid Society, its income would apparently be far larger than it is.

The Committee never included as a part of the Society's income, any sums locally raised to supplement grants or paid by incumbents, to meet grants.

The Quarterly Paper No. CVI., for January, 1876, recorded the decease of the Rev. Dr. Harding, formerly Bishop of Bombay, and the first energetic and valuable Honorary Secretary of the Society, and Rev. Thomas Vores, of St. Mary's, Hastings.

The Quarterly Paper No. CVII., for April, 1876, recorded the decease of the Rev. Thomas Hill, Archdeacon of Derby, an old and very liberal supporter of the Society.

The Committee stated that it was greatly to be desired that many more of the clergy would offer themselves for the work of "Special Missions." It was impossible that the same men could go to every place where a preacher was required, or be away from their parishes more than once or twice in the year, even if they could bear the physical fatigue connected with these special duties. The Committee sincerely hoped that those who were suited for these Evangelistic services would send in their names to the Society.

The Forty-second Annual Meeting was held in St. James's Hall, London, on Thursday, 3rd of May, 1877, the Earl of Shaftesbury, K.G., in the chair. The speakers were the Bishop of Gloucester and Bristol, the Revs. James Fleming, B.D., Canon Garbett, D. Howell, T. A. Stowell, and N. D. J. Straton, and Sir T. F. Buxton, Bart., and Mr. Philip Vernon Smith. The sermon was preached in St. Dunstan's Church, Fleet Street, London, on the 2nd of May, 1877, by Archdeacon Prest, upon the text Nehemiah iv. 20.

The Report recorded the decease of Mr. Justice Archibald, Messrs John Sperling and H. V. Tebbs, old, valuable, and much-respected members of the Committee. Also of Mrs. Reginald Smith, Stafford Rectory, Dorchester, who for many years was one of the mainsprings of the Society in the county Dorset, and by her zeal and great exertions raised up many friends on its behalf.

Reviewing the "baneful evil of unbelief," the Committee offered the following suggestions :—

1. For want of teachers of sound religious prin-ciples, many children too often, just at the critical period of their leaving school, fell into the hands of the destroyer through the Sunday newspaper, and the demoralizing periodical, thereby sup-planting all the instruction previously received. The increased advantage of Sunday-schools, not as as mere adjuncts to the day-schools, but as con-

stituting a distinct and independent agency, could not possibly be over-estimated.

2. The extension of lay agency was another most effective means of counteracting the progress of infidelity amongst our town populations.

3. The formation of good lending libraries for the people would be a valuable assistance in repelling the influence of corrupting literature.

INTEMPERANCE.

The Committee remarked that it was very doubtful whether legislation was capable of supplying a sufficient remedy against the sin of drunkenness. As many as 13,584 of the clergy of the Church of England had addressed the Archbishops and Bishops on this subject.

They strongly felt that it was on the transforming influence of the Gospel that the clergy must mainly rely for delivering large numbers of their people from the thraldom by which they were thus held.

In the Quarterly Paper No. CIX., for January, 1877, they remarked that the clergy generally formed a high estimate of the value and importance of their Sunday-schools, but they seemed to think them capable of great improvement. It was a matter of duty and sound policy to improve the teachers and to use every effort by Bible-classes and teachers' meetings to make the existing staff more intelligent, more regular, and above all more spiritual.

Referring to the "Special Mission" movement, the Committee in the Quarterly Paper No. CX., for April, 1877, remarked that the Society had taken an active part in the movement by procuring qualified clergymen of Evangelical sentiments to visit any parish where their services might be required; and also by providing occasionally some small pecuniary assistance when necessary towards the expenses of any Special Mission.

The Forty-third Annual Meeting was held in St. James's Hall, London, on Thursday, 2nd of May, 1878, the Earl of Shaftesbury, K.G., in the chair. The speakers were Bishop Perry; the Revs. A. B. Carpenter, John Ellison, Archdeacon Griffith, J. F. Kitto, Canon Martin; and Viscount Midleton. The sermon was preached in St. Dunstan's Church, Fleet Street, London, by the Bishop of Sodor and Man, upon the words of the Gospel St. Luke x. 1.

The Committee in the Report felt obliged to state that, having regard to the very large number of applications which had been made, and were likely to be made, for grants from the Society towards the expenses of Special Missions, and to the impossibility of responding to them all without unduly trenching upon the regular work of the Society, and to the disappointment and mis- understanding which were caused by the unavoidable refusal of a large number of them, had lately decided that no grants of this description be voted for the future.

The legacies this year included 3,000*l.* from Mr. George Moore, which by the terms of the will was to be invested, and the interest only used for the work of the Society.

The friends of the Society were entreated to bear in mind that the maintenance even of existing grants was dependent upon liberal support being speedily rendered, while the extension of assistance to incumbents waiting for aid would, under present circumstances, needs be indefinitely postponed. Painful would it be to them to withdraw grants or reduce their amount, and the Committee had been anxious not to take this step until the latest possible moment; but it was now evident that this must be done to the extent of between 8,000*l.* and 9,000*l.*, involving, perhaps, the withdrawal of upwards of *one hundred* grants, if within the next two or three months additional means were not provided.

The attention of those incumbents who received aid was called to the necessity of using their best efforts to increase their remittances.

GRANTS TO LARGE TOWNS.

The following table showed the number of grants of some of our large provincial towns, including the parish of Islington, in London, and their cost to the Society, together with the aggregate returns made by those towns, for the year ending 31st March, 1877.

PLACE	Population benefited	Curates.	Grants to Lay-agents.	Cost to the Society.	Amounts returned to Society during year ending Mar. 31, 1877.			Per-centage of cost returned to Society.
				£	£	s.	d.	
Birmingham	333,535	30	25	4,630	1,315	1	8	28
Liverpool	290,485	26	7	2,895	2,002	13	5	69
Manchester	274,600	21	20	2,930	1,531	8	3	52
Islington, London...	160,520	15	7	1,950	640	8	10	32
Sheffield	133,894	14	3	1,500	891	19	3	59
Bradford	113,683	17	4	1,790	436	0	2	24
Blackburn............	95,694	12	2	1,330	370	13	7	27
Nottingham	94,385	13	5	1,490	739	11	1	49
Leeds.................	89,749	12	3	1,240	422	7	4	34
Newcastle-on-Tyne .	89,000	8	1	810	227	8	6	28
Bristol	80,538	14	1	1,270	1,098	18	11	86·
Hull	69,155	9	3	920	388	12	1	42

The Quarterly Paper No. CXI., for October, 1877, stated that after all that of late years had been done in the subdivision of parishes, there were still many of unwieldy size and overgrown population. Out of the 709 parishes aided by the Society, no fewer than 139 contained populations of 10,000 and upwards. They were thus classified :—

50 parishes of 10,000		3 parishes of 20,000
24 „ 11,000	1 „	23,000
17 „ 12,000	1 „	24,000
12 „ 13,000	1 „	25,000
8 „ 14,000	3 „	26,000
10 „ 15,000	——	
8 „ 16,000	139	
1 „ 18,000	——	

The populations of the remaining parishes, with few exceptions, ranged from 4,000 to 10,000, the average being about 7,000 to each incumbent.

It was suggested in October, 1877, that the Quarterly Paper might be made more generally useful by being thrown into the shape of a magazine, not confined to matters bearing directly on the work of the Church Pastoral-Aid Society, but occasionally introducing stories drawn from city and village life, embracing short and pithy articles, details of religious work of all kinds, a page for questions and answers, and tales judiciously written and bearing more or less directly on pastoral work. Such a quarterly magazine might be sold at threepence or sixpence. The Committee gave their full attention to these suggestions, but they did not see their way to adopt them. In this day of numerous publications, when many parishes had their local magazine, they very much questioned whether a new one was at all requisite, or would meet with acceptance. Their present publication was a business paper, and was much valued by many who took' an interest in the Society's work.

FINANCIAL DIFFICULTY.

The Quarterly Paper No. CXII., for January, 1878, contained the following statement on this subject :—At no former period was there greater reason for urgently pleading for an increase of funds. That the financial position of the Society is serious will appear from the fact that the income for the year ending the 31st of March last fell short of the expenditure by 5,302l. If there should be, as is but too probable, a deficiency of anything like that amount during the current year, the Committee would be constrained to reduce their existing operations, a measure so disastrous that they scarcely venture to contemplate its possibility. In order to meet the quarterly payments on the 21st of November, it was necessary to draw on the " Contingency Fund " for 5,000l. The Committee are thankful that by the wise foresight and liberality of their late friend, Mr. John Bockett, there was such a reserve to fall back upon in their present financial embarrassment, but this sum must be replaced out of the first money received.

It is most desirable that this small fund—now
only 5,000*l.*—should be increased instead of
diminished, for in addition to the difficulty arising
from the outlay being at any time above the
income, the Society's *liabilities*, in excess of its
actual expenditure, are very great, inasmuch as
many grants which are now unoccupied might at
an early date be filled up.   They therefore earnestly
plead for a large increase in those reliable sources
of income—subscriptions and collections in
churches and at meetings—in order that the
Society might not be crippled in its action, or the
applications on the list for aid, already both
numerous and urgent, accumulate even still more.

WORK ON CANALS.

In previous Reports and Papers attention had
been drawn to the provision which the Society
made for our canal population.   At Runcorn,
Gloucester, and Worcester, special efforts had
been made for the religious and moral benefit
of boatmen and bargemen.   Foremost in this
benevolent movement was the late Rev. John
Davies.

The Watermen's Church at Worcester was
eventually called the "Davies Memorial Church,"
and the Committee stated that as circumstances
arose which seem to change its character, causing it
to be more of a district church than one specially for

boatmen, and as the departure of both vicar and curate who had taken a lively interest in the work occurred at this time, they felt that this special grant was not necessary.

There were numerous other parishes through which canals passed. In many of these the boatmen and their families were benefited by the Society's agency.

The Quarterly Paper No. CXIII., for April, 1878, drew attention to the work of the Society in the mining and colliery districts. To localities of this character several of the earliest grants were made.

The Forty-fourth Annual Meeting was held in the Freemasons' Hall, London, on Thursday, 8th of May, 1879, the Earl of Shaftesbury, K.G., in the chair. The speakers were the Bishop of Gloucester and Bristol and Bishop Ryan; the Revs. B. Cassin, J. McCormick, and A. Oates; the Earls of Aberdeen and Chichester, and Mr. J. M. Holt, M.P. The sermon was preached in St. Dunstan's Church, Fleet Street, London, on the 7th of May, 1879, by the Bishop of Rochester, upon the text Ephesians i. 7, 9, 19, 22, 23.

The Report recorded the decease of Mr. Thomas Graham, an old and much-respected member of the Committee.

CHURCH BUILDING.

It was stated, that of the 14,077 existing churches, chapels, and other buildings belonging to the Church of England there were built—

Before 1801 ...	...	9667
Between 1801—1811 ...	...	55
,, 1811—1821 ...	...	97
,, 1821—1831 ...	...	276
,, 1831—1841 ...	...	667
,, 1841—1851 ...	...	1197
Dates not mentioned ...	...	2118

In the last twenty years and more the building and endowing of churches had proceeded upon a scale altogether unprecedented. A new estimate of the places of worship would show how marvellous had been the increase during that period. Through the agency of the Society alone 339 churches had been erected and 339 rooms were used for Divine service, most of which would in due time end in the permanent structure.

SPECIAL APPEAL.

The following Appeal was issued by the Committee and inserted in the newspapers :—" *The Committee beg to call the serious attention of their friends and the public generally to the present critical position of the Society, and to state that the total available income for the year ending 31st of*

March, 1878, has fallen short of the expenditure by 8,500l. The maintenance, therefore, of the Society's grants is entirely dependent upon liberal support being speedily rendered. The Committee will otherwise be compelled to adopt the painful alternative of withdrawing probably upwards of one hundred grants, to the amount of nearly 9,000l. It will be evident that the extension of assistance to incumbents who are anxiously awaiting aid, must, under present circumstances, be postponed."

The response to this Appeal was not such as to afford any reasonable prospect of equalising the income and expenditure of the Society during the year. The alternative seemed to be between the withdrawal of 100 grants or reducing every grant.

ASSOCIATION SECRETARIES—THEIR DUTIES AND DIFFICULTIES.

The Committee remarked in their Quarterly Paper No. CXIV., for October, 1878, that the question of the employment of Association Secretaries was no longer one of opinion or theory; it had been proved by experience to be absolutely necessary.

The duties of these officers were thus summarized: —

" To be performed at Home."

1. Applying every year to those who either occasionally or regularly gave sermons or held

meetings on behalf of the Society asking them to name some convenient day in the year.

2. Forwarding annually a circular to the clergy in his district, soliciting their support of the Society, enclosing at the same time copies of suitable papers and circulars from the office in London, and making a similar appeal to all newly appointed incumbents.

3. Dealing with the answers to the several applications which had been made by arranging for the sermons and meetings proposed during the current year.

4. Securing deputations for those places which the Association Secretary himself is unable to visit.

5. Preparation and delivery of sermons and lectures, and writing special circulars adapted to local distribution.

" Duties entailing absence from Home."

1. Preaching on Sunday, and, when sermons could be arranged, on week evenings.

2. Lecturing or attending meetings during the week.

3. Calling on clergymen and laymen in the neighbourhood of the parish in which the Association Secretary had been preaching, to canvass them. A personal visit was found to be far more effective than a letter.

4. Arranging for sermons in two or three different churches on the same Sunday, or for lectures on consecutive nights in the same neighbourhood.

5. Visiting the parishes of grantees in order to obtain for the guidance of the Committee information respecting the working of their grants.

THE ASSOCIATION SECRETARIES' DIFFICULTIES.

1. They found that they did not obtain to the extent that might be expected the support of the large body of the Evangelical clergy.

2. Their inability to arrange for sermons and meetings in several neighbouring parishes at the same time.

3. While some grantees gave most valuable assistance as deputations, others were very backward in going out to preach for the Society.

DAY OF SUPPLICATION WITH THANKSGIVING.

An opinion having been expressed that there should be united supplication for Home as well as Foreign Missions, the Committee suggested that Wednesday, the 19th of February, the anniversary of the day on which the Society was instituted in 1836, should be observed as a day of supplication with thanksgiving, and they hoped on that day, at ten o'clock, to assemble and meet the members and friends of the Society at its offices

in Falcon Court, Fleet Street, London. The
Committee felt sure that their clerical friends
throughout the country would arrange for parochial
meetings for this purpose.

The Committee and some of their friends
accordingly assembled at the Society's offices on
the date above mentioned. The chair was occupied
by the Earl of Shaftesbury, K.G., President of
the Society.

The Secretary commenced the proceedings by
reading the 46th Psalm, and the Rev. J. H. Moran
offered up prayer. After singing a hymn, Mr.
John Martin read St. Matthew ix. 35—38, and
Acts xx. 28—35, and the Rev. Prebendary Auriol
offered up prayer for a greater number of faithful
labourers. Mr. C. H. Bousfield read Philippians i.,
and the Rev. Canon Reeve prayed that many
might be stirred up to assist the Society in the
glorious work in which it is engaged. Mr. Philip
Vernon Smith read 1 Chron. xxix. 10—19, and
the Rev. Thomas Nolan, D.D., offered thanksgiving for all the good which God had wrought
through this special agency. A hymn was then
sung, after which the Chairman, in the course of
a brief address, said that forty-three years ago on
that day he occupied the chair, and assisted in
the foundation of the Society. Two or three
smaller meetings had been previously held in the
locality in which he and his friends assembled.

o

Of those present at those meetings there were only three survivors, two of whom were now present. He viewed the Society's present financial difficulty as only a trial of their faith. The Society was a thousand times more necessary now than on the day it was first established, and he could not believe that it would be suffered to decline.

The circular of invitation for a special observance of the day had been largely distributed throughout the country, and met with a hearty response from the incumbents of many of the most important parishes aided in which appropriate sermons were preached and meetings held.

Many suggestions as to the best means of increasing the Society's funds were made to the Committee at this time. The Bishop of Gloucester and Bristol, in his speech at the anniversary meeting, expressed the opinion that there was hardly sufficient co-operative organization in the different country dioceses; "at any rate," said the Bishop, " I can speak for my own diocese, and I think that a very few alterations in local arrangements would really have the effect of bringing together, at certain times, all the friends of the Society for a grand united effort. . . . . What I mean to do is, to ask the Organizing Secretaries to do me the great kindness and favour of coming to me to confer with me in reference to this

Society. . . . . I intend, if God shall spare me till the autumn, to confer with your Organizing and Local Secretaries in my diocese. I really do think that a very small amount of pressure will bring from us, at any rate, such a contribution as will reduce the ten per cent. reduction to five per cent. in the next year; and if our indefatigable Secretary will only send round to the Vice-Presidents and other friends, and to all who are connected officially with this Society, a hearty reminder that we had better do what we can in such ways as we think likely to prove the best, I am sure that appeal will be very largely responded to."

The Forty-fifth Annual Meeting was held in St. James's Hall, Piccadilly, London, on Thursday, 6th of May, 1880, the Earl of Shaftesbury, K.G., in the chair. The speakers were the Revs. F. S. Cook, J. G. Dixon, T. H. Gill, John Richardson, Dr. Ryle, J. A. Smith, and Sir W. T. Charley, Q.C., D.C.L. The sermon was preached in St. Dunstan's Church, Fleet Street, London, on the 5th May, 1880, by the Rev. Canon John Richardson, upon the text Nehemiah vi. 9.

The Report recorded the decease of Dr. Baring, Bishop of Durham, a Vice-President of the Society. His successor, Dr. Lightfoot, had accepted the office of Vice-President.

BOARD SCHOOLS.

Whilst admitting that the spread of education under School Board auspices was generally such as to inspire feelings of thankfulness, the Committee remarked that they could not but regard with far greater pleasure the proofs furnished by the educational statistics of the efficacy of the Voluntary system, which secured distinctly Christian instruction.

SUPPLY OF CLERGY.

The Report stated that the utmost vigilance was exercised by the Committee to secure the services of men holding firmly to the distinctive truths of Holy Scripture, and thoroughly loyal to the principles of the Reformation. It seemed quite unnecessary at this period to say that from its institution such had ever been the views of the Society. This was shown during the past year in a case which attracted attention, and created some opposition and caused the wisdom of the Committee to be in some degree called in question. They felt, however, persuaded that the right and only course for them to pursue was to maintain its original principles in all their integrity.

SWANSEA CASE.

The opposition to the Society above alluded to arose out of what was known as "The Swansea

Case." In October, 1879, several letters reached the Committee from warm friends of the Society, expressing their great astonishment that Father Benson, one of the Cowley Fathers, had, during the Congress at Swansea, preached twice in Christ Church in that town, which was aided by a grant from the Society for a curate. The writers expressed their hope that immediate action would be taken on a subject so detrimental to the Society's interests, and likely to injure it amongst its supporters.

The Secretary replied to these letters, showing that the Society had no cognizance of such a step ; and that the question should, at the earliest moment, be brought before the Committee.

Prominent clergymen in the Principality pointed out the absolute necessity of dealing with the case at once, as the church in question was the centre of men of extreme views, one of the wardens being a member of the " English Church Union."

Without fully entering into the several discussions on the subject, it was decided at the General Committee of the 6th October, 1879, that the grant be suspended. Some members felt that in this case there was a legal difficulty, inasmuch as the grant was made, not out of the general funds, but in consequence of a legacy of 300l. bequeathed to the Society towards the support of a curate in that parish.

It was decided, however, that the selection of the
Society by the testator to receive the conditional
bequest indicated his desire that the gift should
be applied in a manner only conformable to the
Society's Protestant and Evangelical principles
and practices.

The grant which previously to this had caused correspondence ceased on the 1st of February, 1880,
and it was resolved that the balance of the Christ
Church Swansea Fund, 129*l*., should be kept in
reserve with interest until such time as the Committee might think it proper to revive the grant.
Some persons were displeased at what they
termed the narrow views of the Society, but the
large body of its supporters throughout the country
approved of the action of the Committee, not only
by commendatory letters, but by liberal contributions.

FUNDS.

To the receipts of the Society this year was
added a donation from Mrs. Disney Robinson,
realising between 4,000*l*. and 5,000*l*., which
had been invested, according to her direction,
in gas shares, to aid in providing curates for five
necessitous parishes in the West Riding of Yorkshire. She made a similar donation in 1875 for
the same purpose.

The funds of the Society, as appeared from the
Quarterly Paper No. CXVIII., for January, 1880,

continued in a very depressed state, and every effort was made to reduce the expenditure. Since April, 1878, numerous grants had been removed from the list, and a continual reduction of at least 10 per cent. had been made in the existing grants as they came up for renewal; and the liabilities of the Society consequently were nearly 11,000*l.* less than on the 1st of April, 1878. But as the greater number of the grants removed from the list were out of operation, the reduction effected would only cause a saving during the year ending 31st of March, 1880, of 5,000*l.* The receipts were already 8,400*l.* less than at the corresponding period 1879, and in the face of that fact it could not be expected that the income to the 31st of March would equal that of the last year.

PROGRESS OF INCOME AND GRANTS.

The following tabular statement exhibits the progress of the annual income and grants of the Society :—

Year.	Number of grants.			Income of Society.		
	Curates.	Lay agents.	Total.	£	s.	d.
1839	167	26	193	10,400	0	0
1849	274	78	352	32,005	12	1
1859	391	154	545	43,856	15	3
1869	537	192	729	51,845	9	11
1879	560	207	767	56,644	17	10

DISNEY ROBINSON GRANTS.

The Committee, in the Quarterly Paper No. CXVIII., for January, 1880, after stating that the sum of 5,000*l.*, the gift of Mrs. Robinson, had been invested, in accordance with her wish, in the names of trustees, with a view to assist the Society in making five additional grants towards the support of curates in parishes or districts in the West Riding of Yorkshire, stated that five parishes were selected, to each of which a grant of 50*l.* from the Society's General Fund and 50*l.* from the Disney Robinson Memorial Fund was made, to meet 50*l.* raised locally. At the close of the last financial year there remained a balance of 394*l.* to the credit of that Fund arising from grants for curates in the parishes aided being at times out of operation. A further sum of 20*l.* from the balance was, at Mrs. Robinson's desire, added to each of these grants, so long as the balance was available for this purpose, on condition that 50*l.* was raised locally by each of the incumbents; thus making a stipend of 170*l.*, in order to secure the aid of experienced curates, and to retain them in their curacies.

In February, 1879, Mrs. Disney Robinson expressed her wish to make a *second* memorial gift of 5,000*l.* for additional grants in the West Riding of Yorkshire, on condition that every incumbent receiving a grant should be obliged to

add 50*l.* to the curate's stipend from the benefice
or local resources, to meet 50*l.* from her Fund
and 50*l.* from the General Funds of the Society,
making in all 150*l.* a-year. This offer was grate-
fully accepted by the Committee, and in June
last the amount was invested in the names of the
same trustees as those of the former Fund.   Certain parishes were selected from the "list of cases
waiting for aid," inquiry having first been made
whether the incumbents were prepared to comply
with the condition of adding from "local
resources" the sum of 50*l.* to the 50*l.* from the
General Funds of the Society and 50*l.* from the
Disney Robinson Memorial Fund.

MISS F. R. HAVERGAL.

The Committee recorded in this paper the
decease of Miss F. R. Havergal. The circumstances of her early removal invested with a peculiar
interest correspondence with reference to an offer
which she made to the Committee of devoting the
proceeds of the sale of her piano, the gift of her
father, to the funds of the Society. Since her
death the gift (50*l.*) was received.

THE CHURCH IN WALES.

The Quarterly Paper No. CXIX., for April, 1880,
contained observations on two articles which had
recently appeared in the *Churchman* on the state
of the Church in Wales. The Committee
remarked that the difficulty of serving churches

P

separated by wide tracts of country pressed heavily
on many Welsh incumbents.

The Rev. T. H. Hughes, Association Secretary
for Wales, issued a special circular to the clergy
of the Principality, calling their serious attention
to the deficiency in the Society's receipts. Mr.
Hughes remarked that " of the eighty-four applications for aid, many of a very pressing character
come from Wales. The incumbents are anxiously
waiting for assistance, but it is impossible for the
Committee to relieve them until the Society's
funds admit of an increase of operations. Under
these circumstances I venture to hope that a great
and successful effort will be made in every parish
in Wales, especially where there is a grant, to return
a substantial sum to the Society before its financial
year closes."

CONCLUSION.

From the foregoing brief historical sketch of the
Society it will be abundantly evident that it is a
Church of England Society, regarding the wants
of the Church on the one hand, and observing the
order of the Church on the other. It is matter for
great thankfulness and encouragement to all loyal
Churchmen to know that during the past forty-
five years it has been engaged in supporting
clergymen who faithfully hold to the true inter-
pretation of the formularies, discipline, and doctrine of the Established Church. If anyone were

to object to the Society as undertaking to inquire from the incumbents the opinions of the curates and lay agents whom they nominate, it must be remembered that it is bound to take care that the funds entrusted to it by the public are applied in accordance with the views of those Protestant and Evangelical friends by whom they are contributed.

It is now no longer a matter of dispute whether organized lay agency should be admitted or not; episcopal authority has declared it to be a necessary supplement to the work of the ministry. The Bishop of Gloucester and Bristol (Dr. Ellicott), in his speech at the Anniversary Meeting in 1872, observed that to the Church Pastoral-Aid Society belongs "the great and lasting honour of having, notwithstanding much opposition at first, invited lay assistants to aid in the blessed work of evangelizing our masses. . . . . There was a time when all men spoke against lay help . . . . but now-a-days there is not a gathering of English Churchmen, be their opinions what they may, whether what are called High, Low, or Broad Church, who do not make that which this Society has ever advocated almost the first subject in all their discussions."

As a comparison is often made between the incomes of the Church Pastoral-Aid Society and the Additional Curates Society, it is desirable to remember that the former only calculates as income sums actually received by the bankers to

the 31st March each year, as these alone con-
stitute its true income.   If to this there be added
23,753*l.* locally contributed to supplement the
grants and 6,300*l.* paid by the Ecclesiastical Commissioners to meet grants, the total sum raised
during ordinary years, when the income is about
55,000*l.*, directly and indirectly would amount to
more than 85,000*l.*   The total receipts since the
formation of the Society have been 1,680,811*l.*
Although the Society has been greatly blessed for
so many years, and made largely instrumental in
assisting the Church of England to meet the
annually increasing spiritual wants of the country,
the need of its agency is not only as necessary now
as when at first it commenced its operations, but
even far more so.

The Noble President at the last Anniversary
concluded his address with the following words:—
" Let us endeavour to remove the blot from the
Church Pastoral-Aid Society that its efforts are
crippled for want of funds, and that, through the
parsimony of its friends, it is not able to respond
to the cry which comes from all parts of the kingdom for ample and immediate assistance, I say,
let us remove the blot so far as in us lies, and let
us implore Almighty God that He would send His
blessing upon the Society and not only fully maintain but greatly increase its life-giving labours."

" I, if I be lifted up from the earth, will draw all men
unto me."—St. John xii. 32.

INDEX.

----◆----

Q

R

C. A. Macintosh, Printer, Great New-street, Fleet-street, London, E.C.

?u

CPSIA information can be obtained at www.ICGtesting.com
Printed in the USA
LVOW04s1758051015

456971LV00022B/1220/P